ColoringBook

By Banana leaves

....

Colorist's Name

....

Date

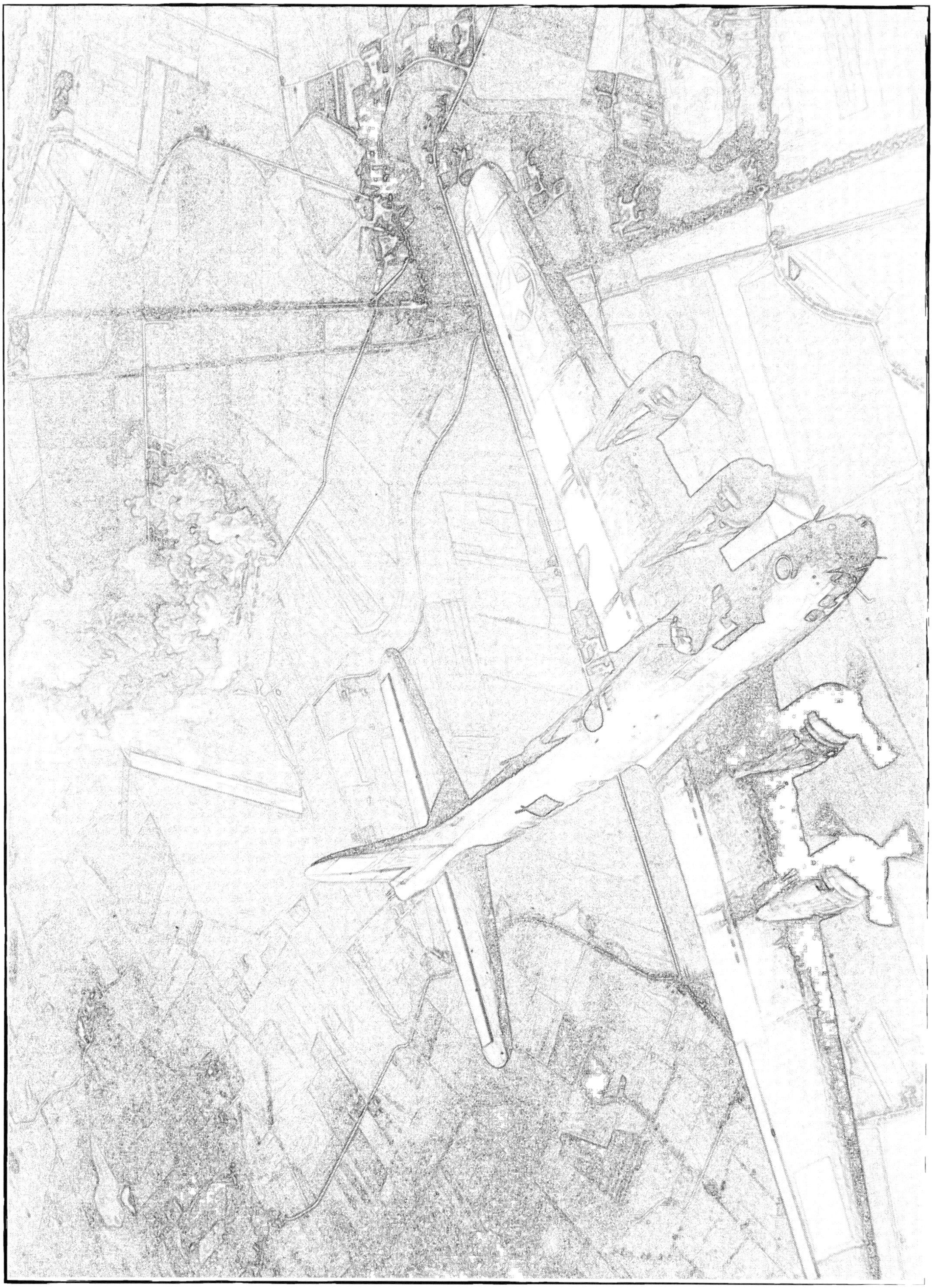

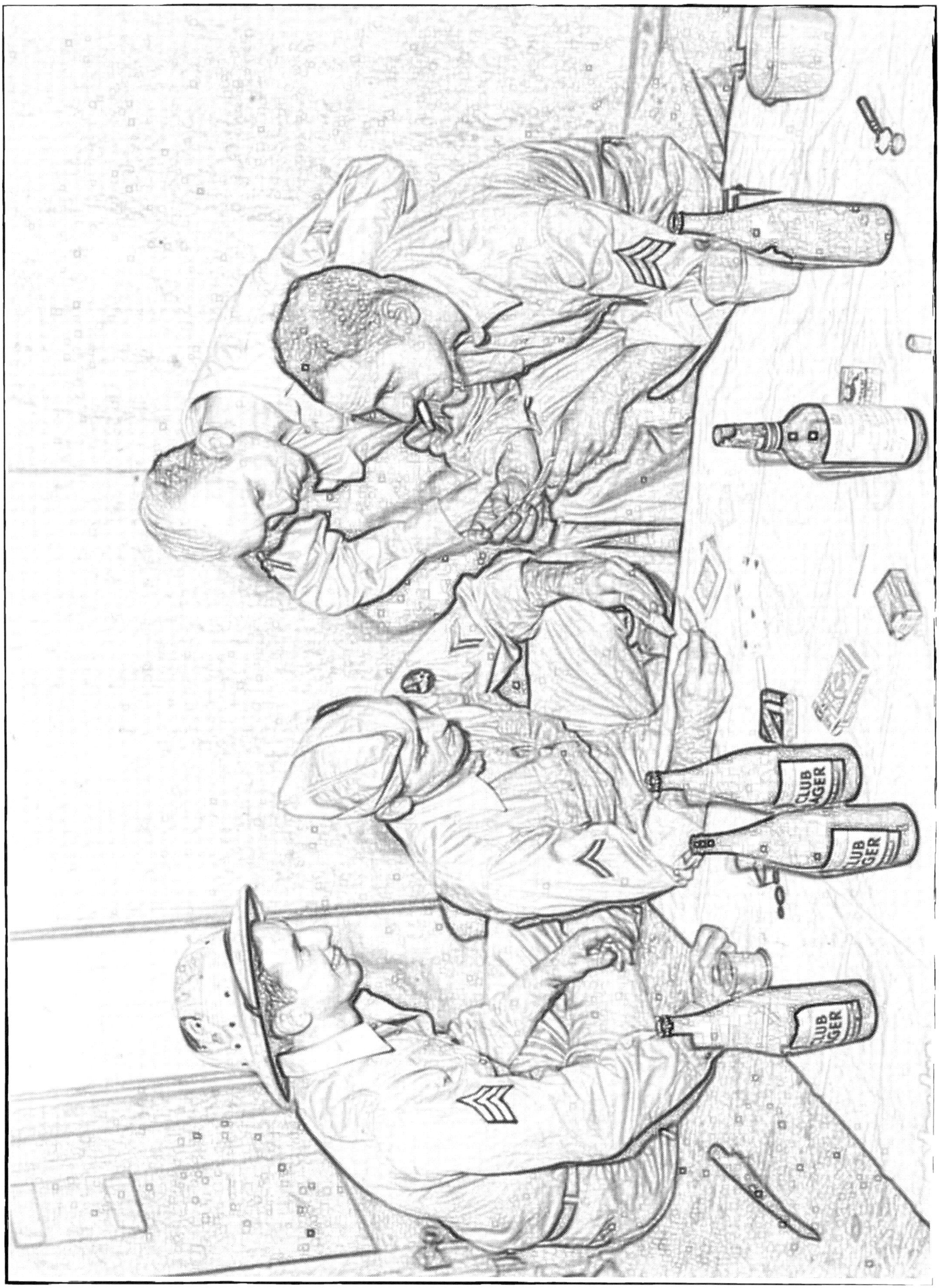
CLUB
AGER

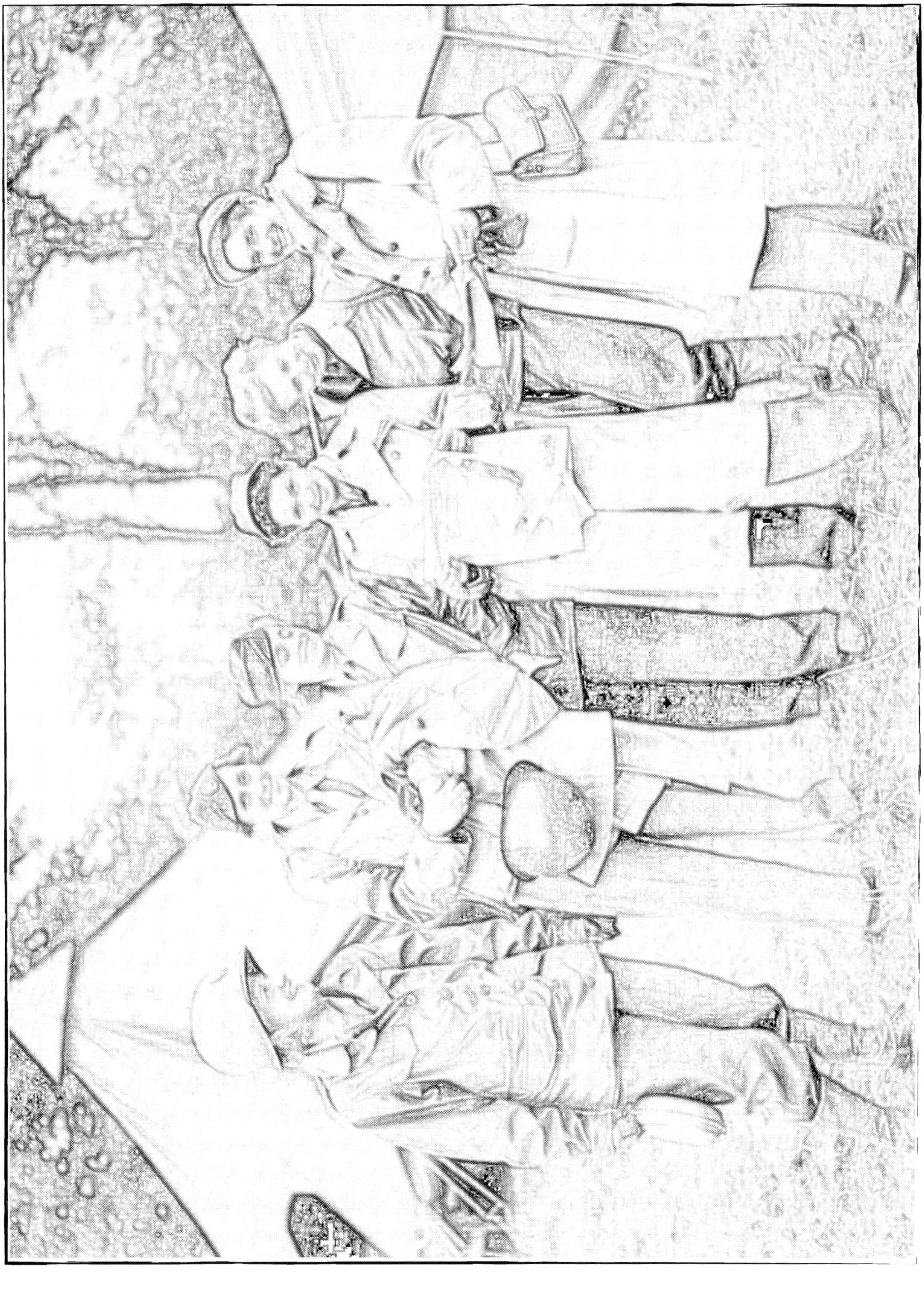

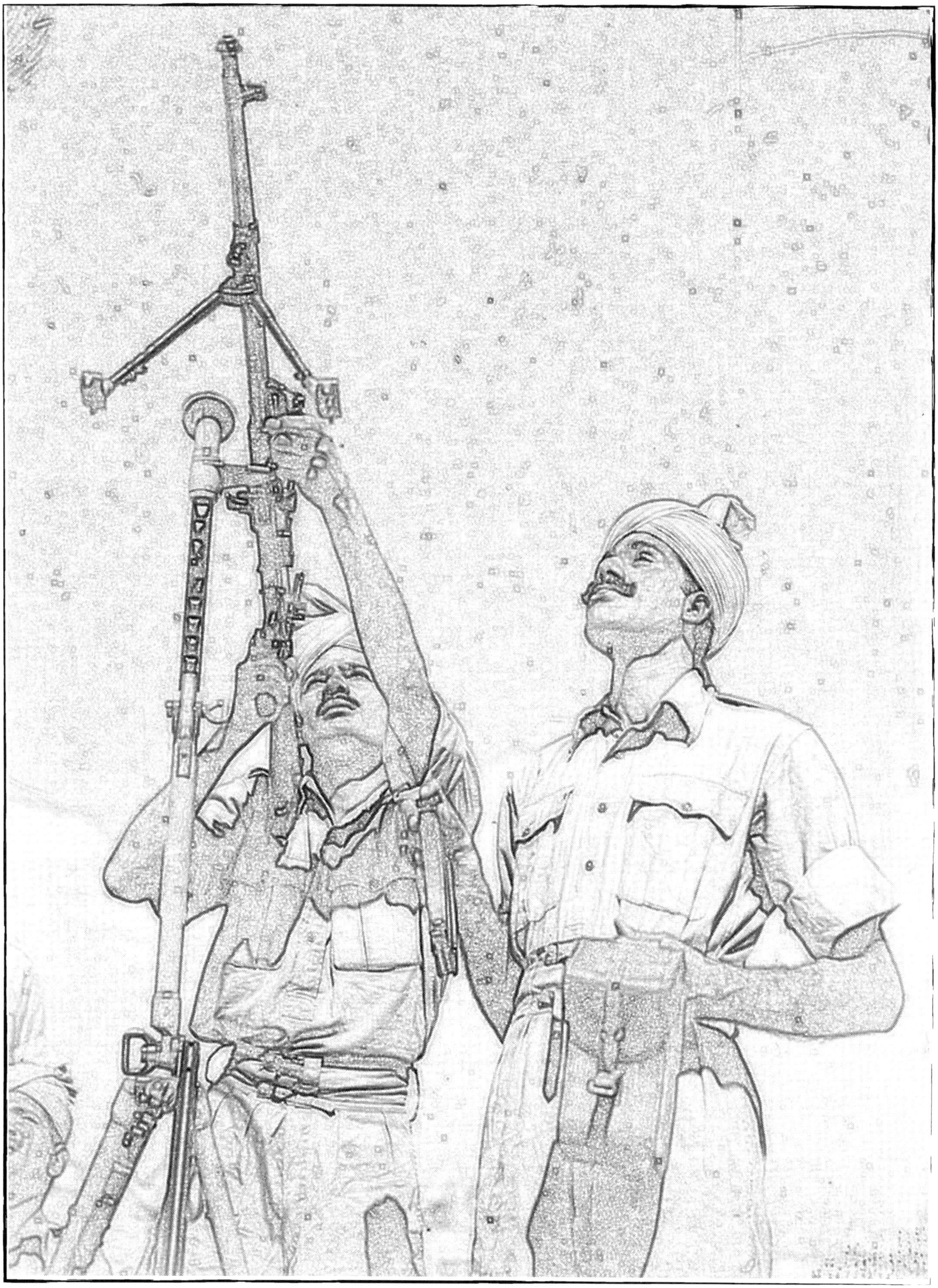

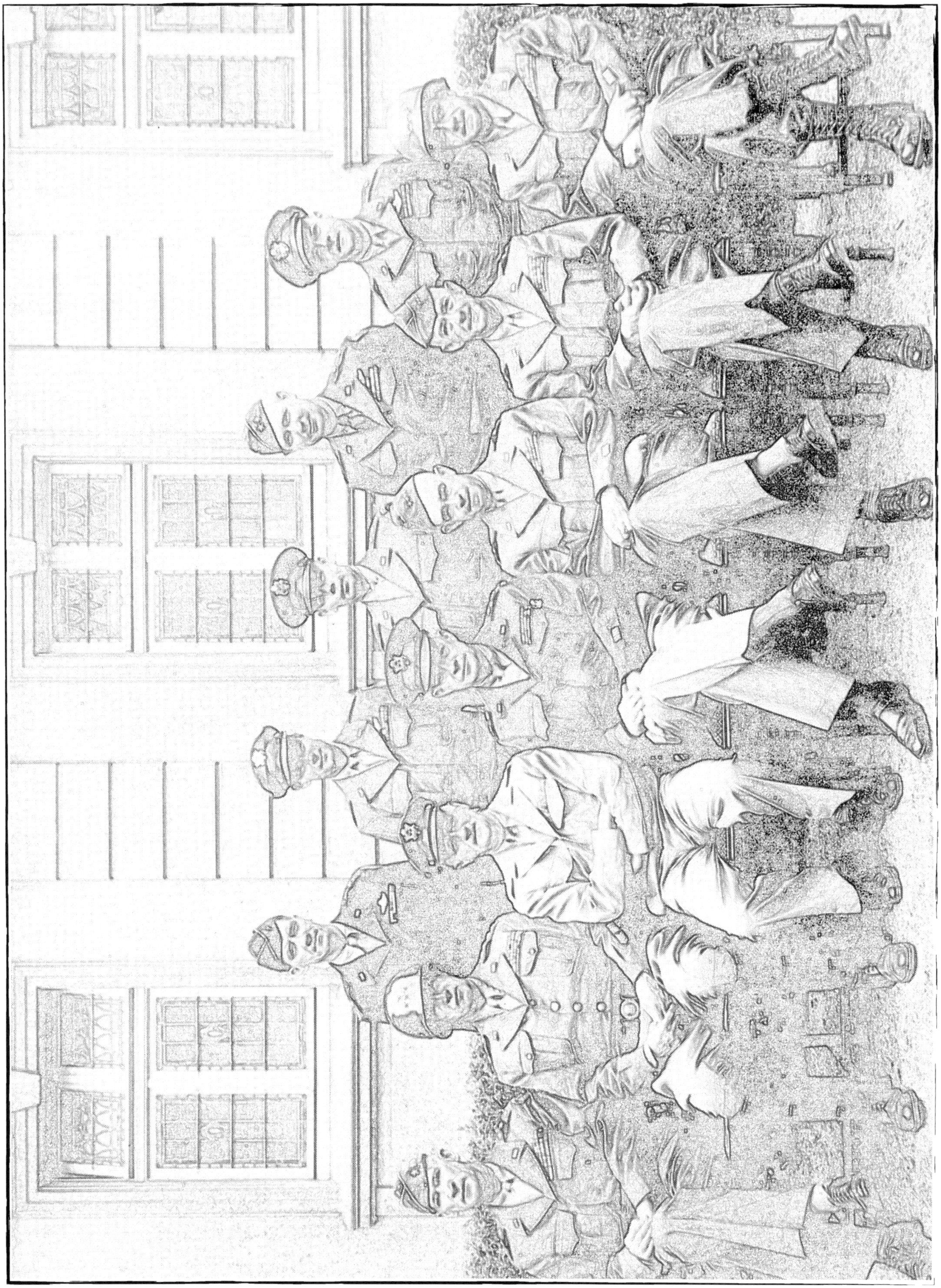

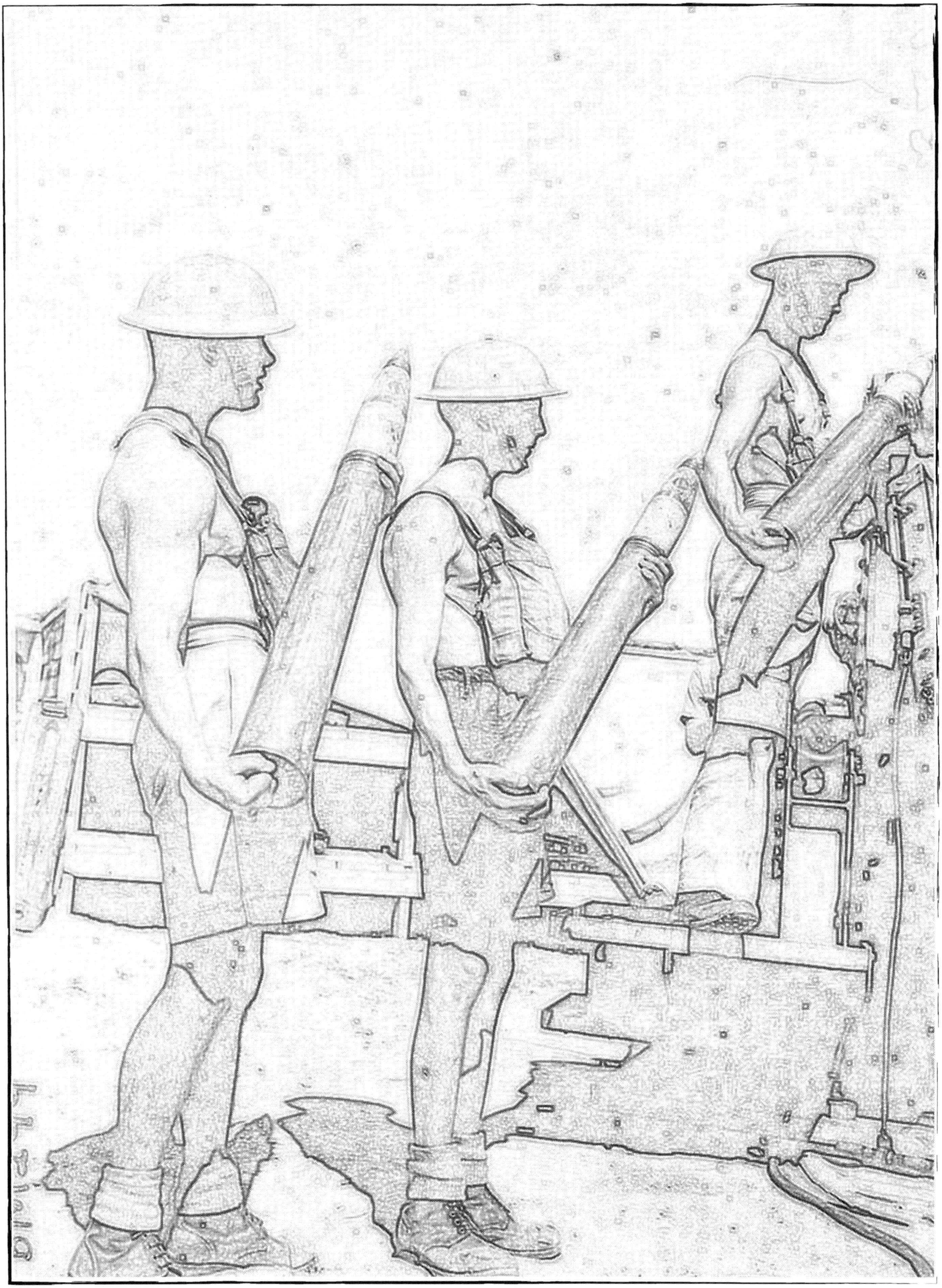

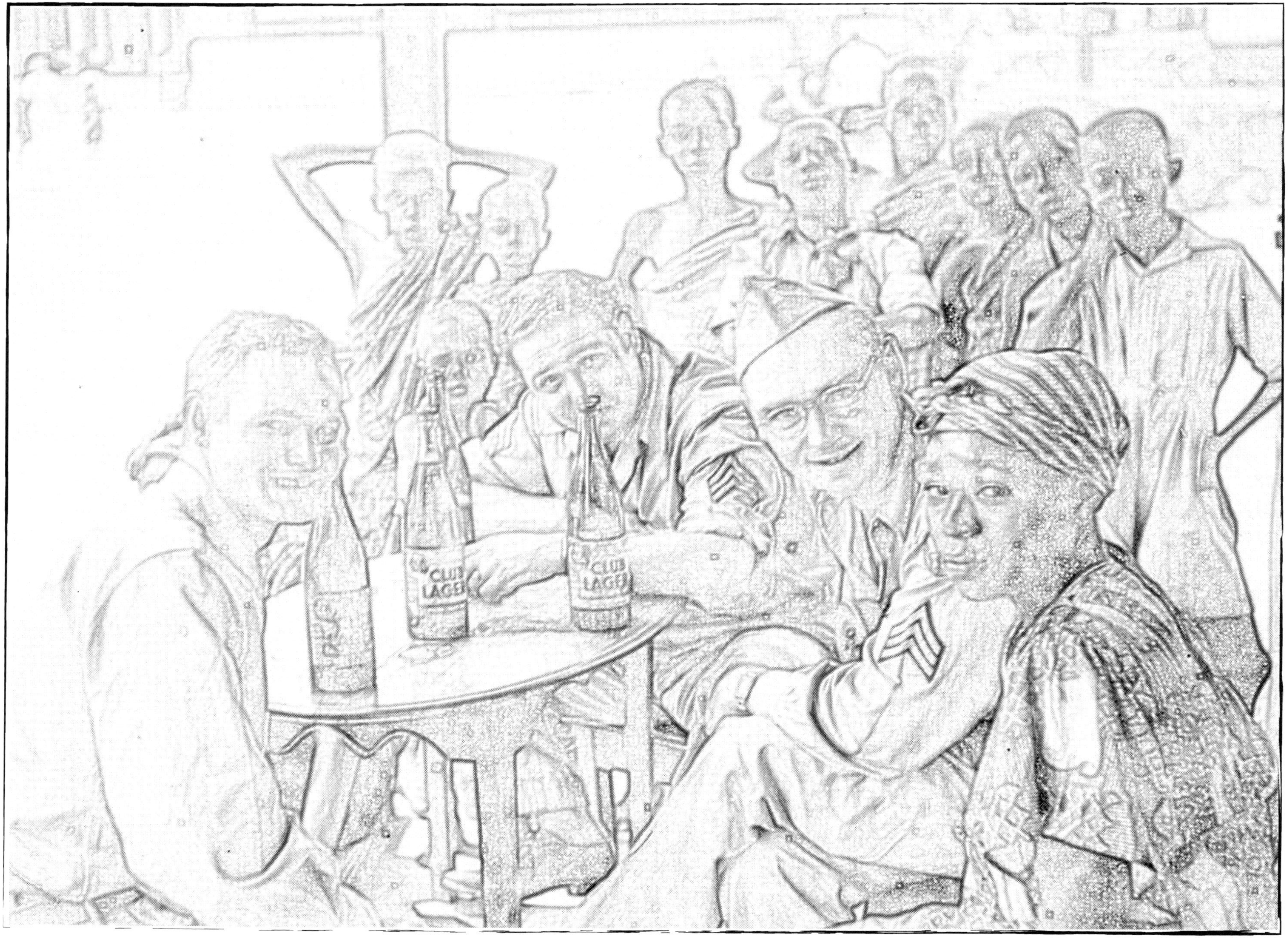
CLUB LAGER

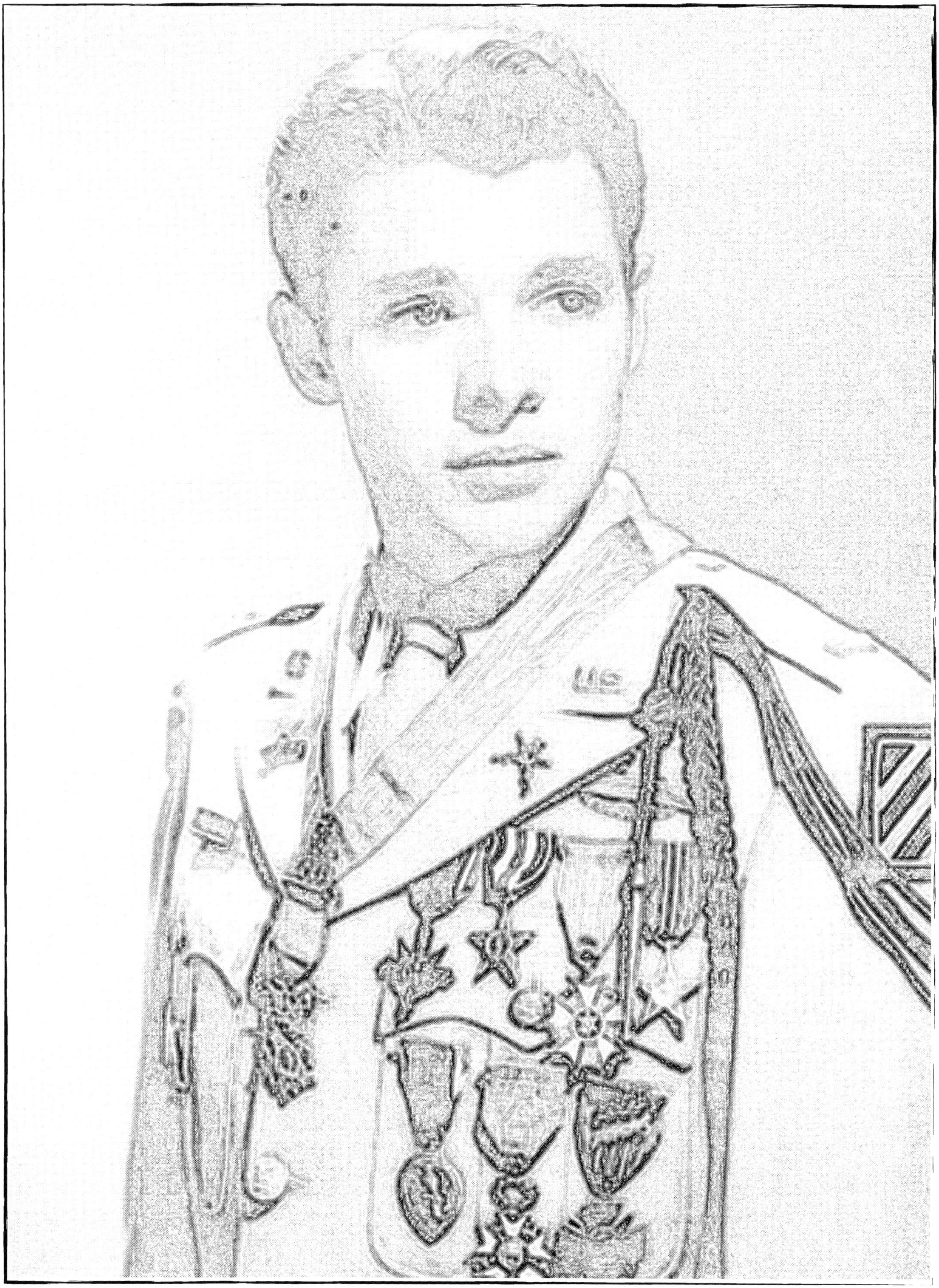
US

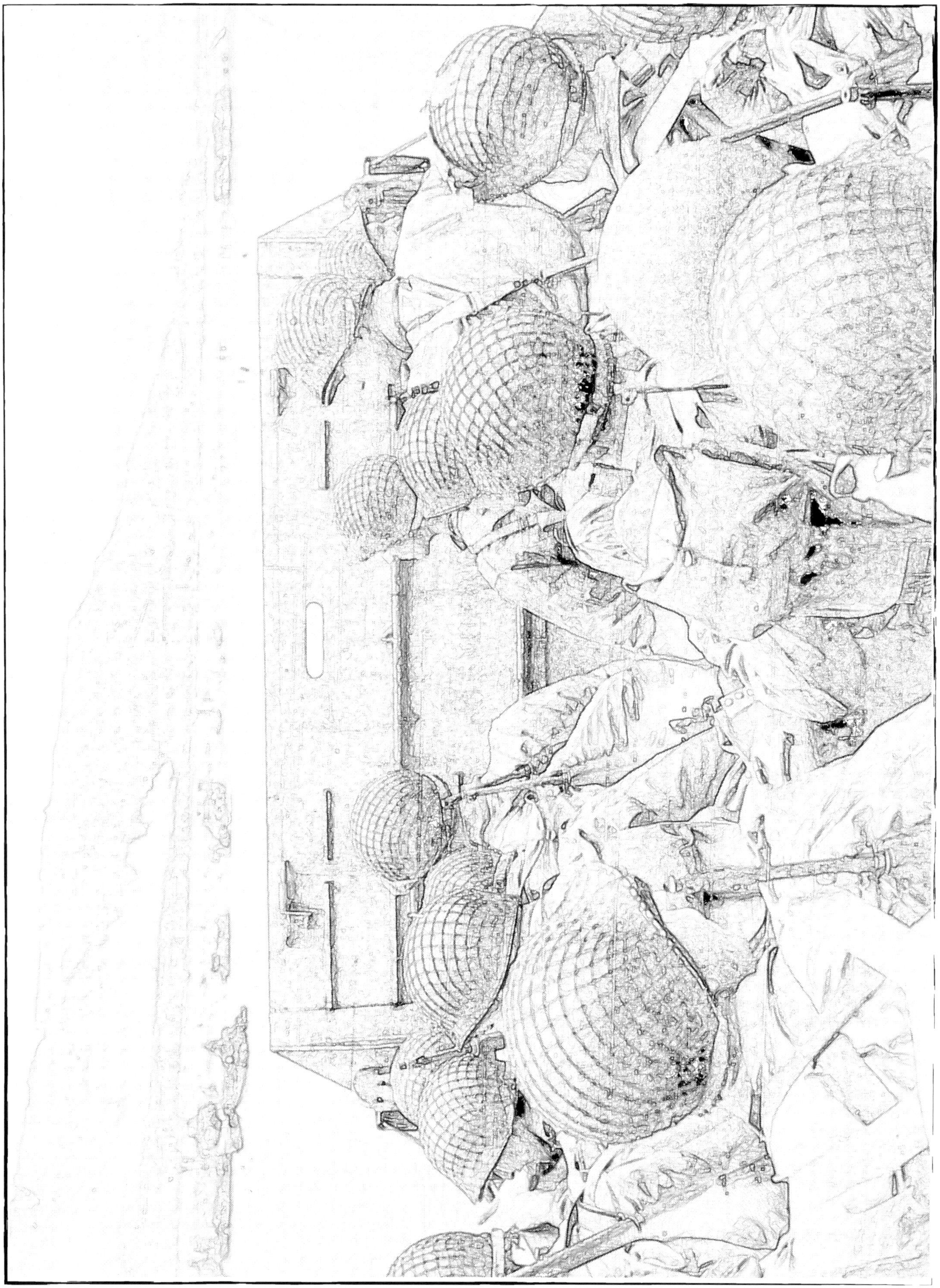

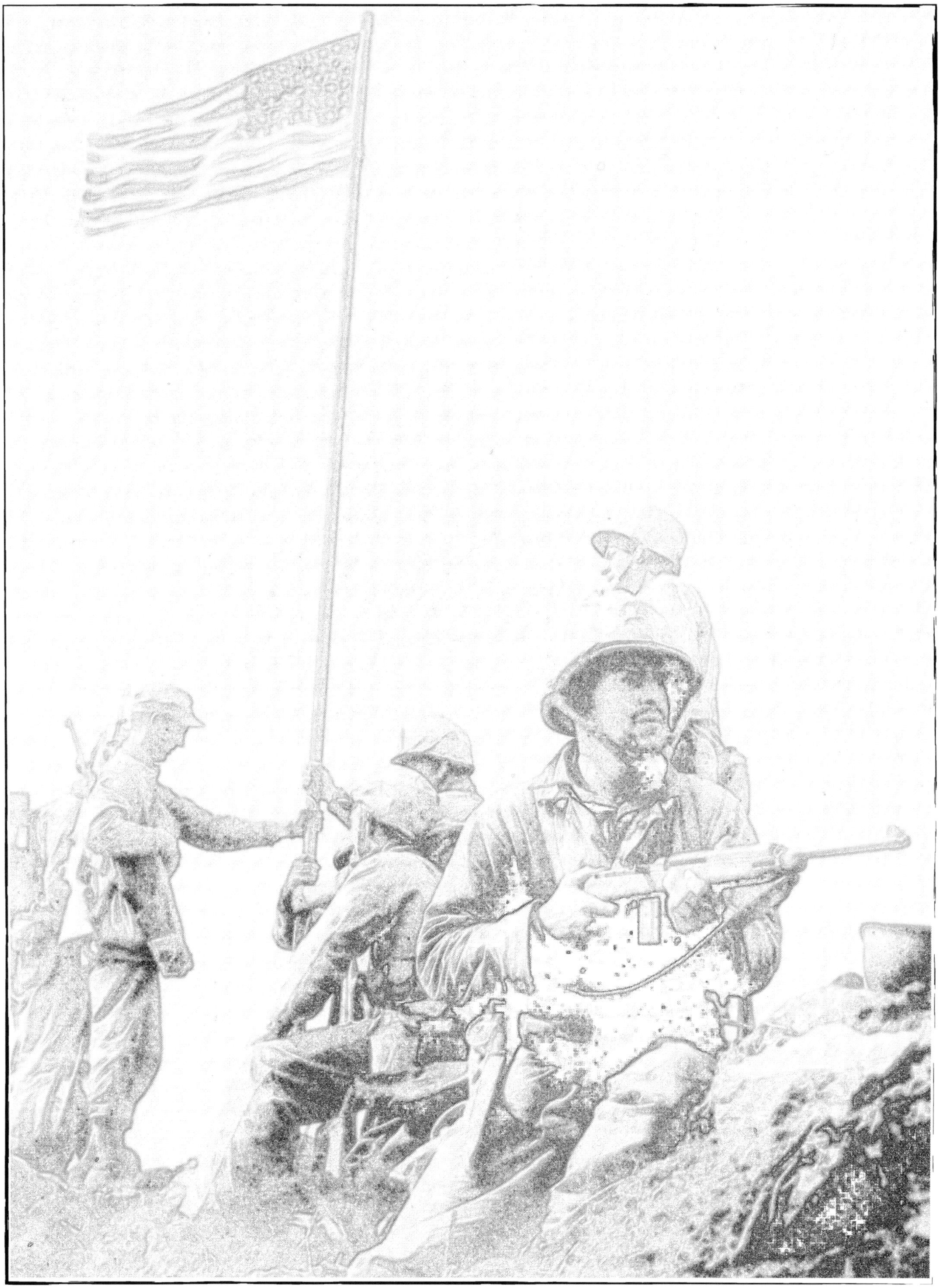

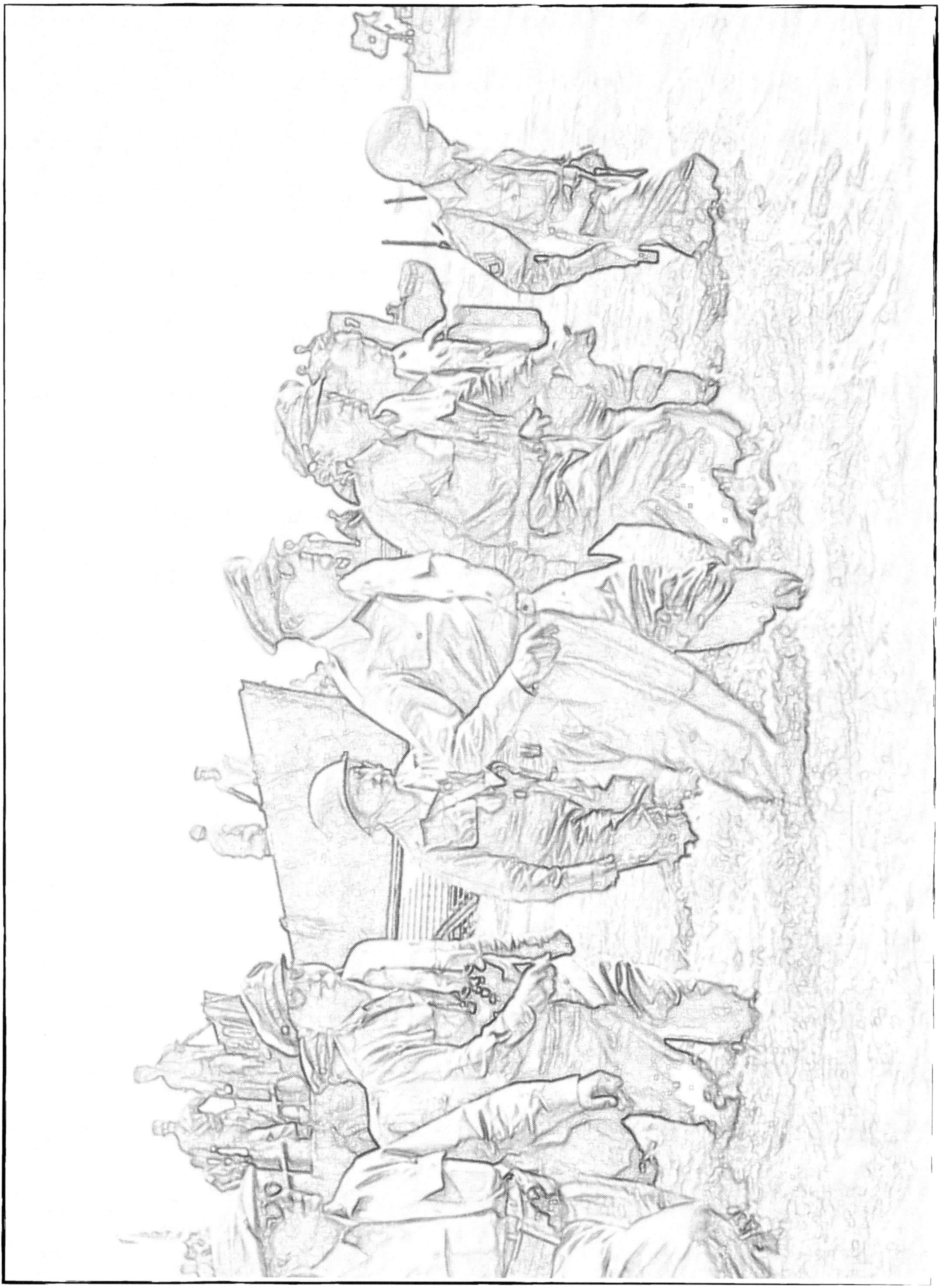

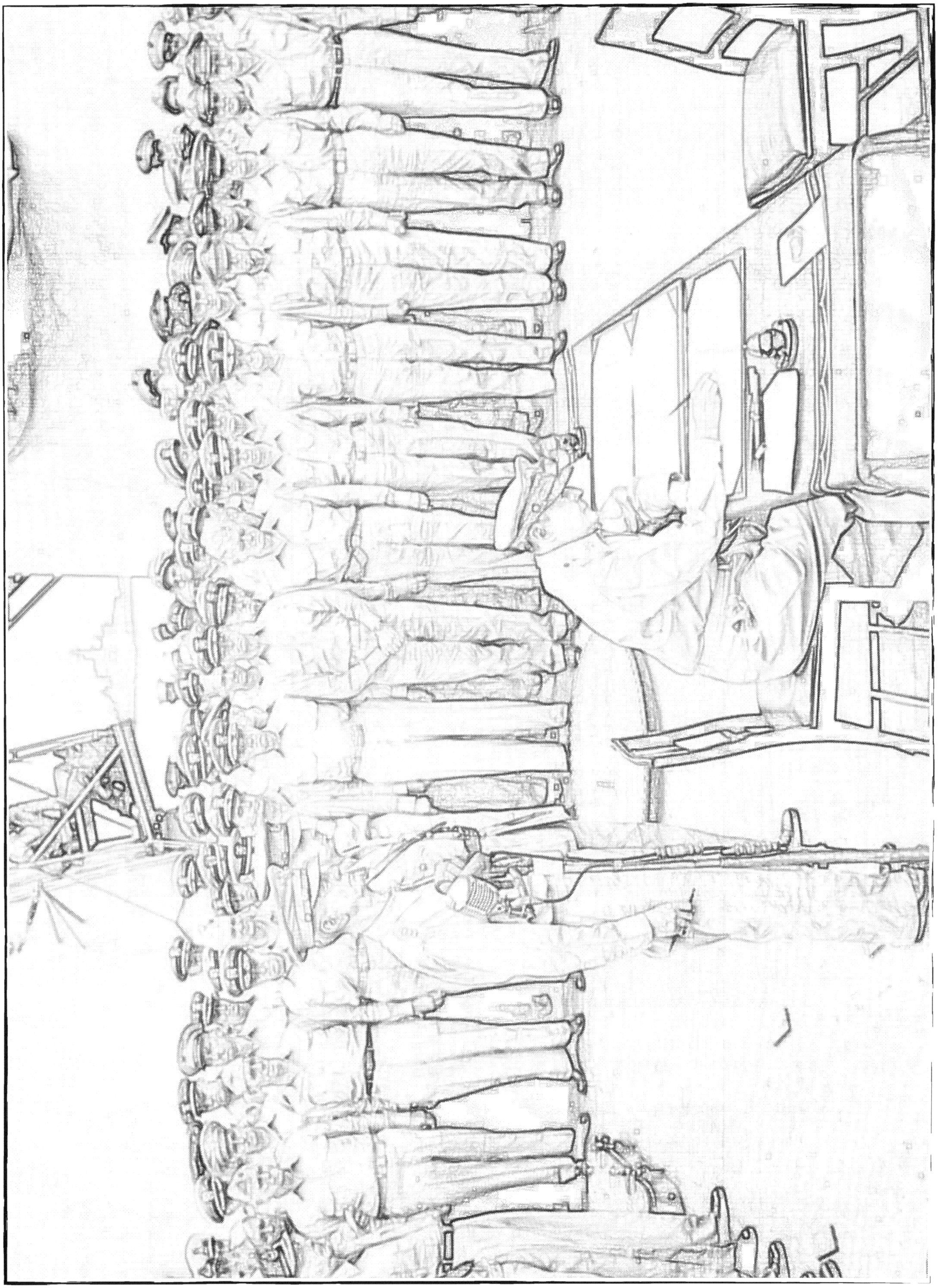

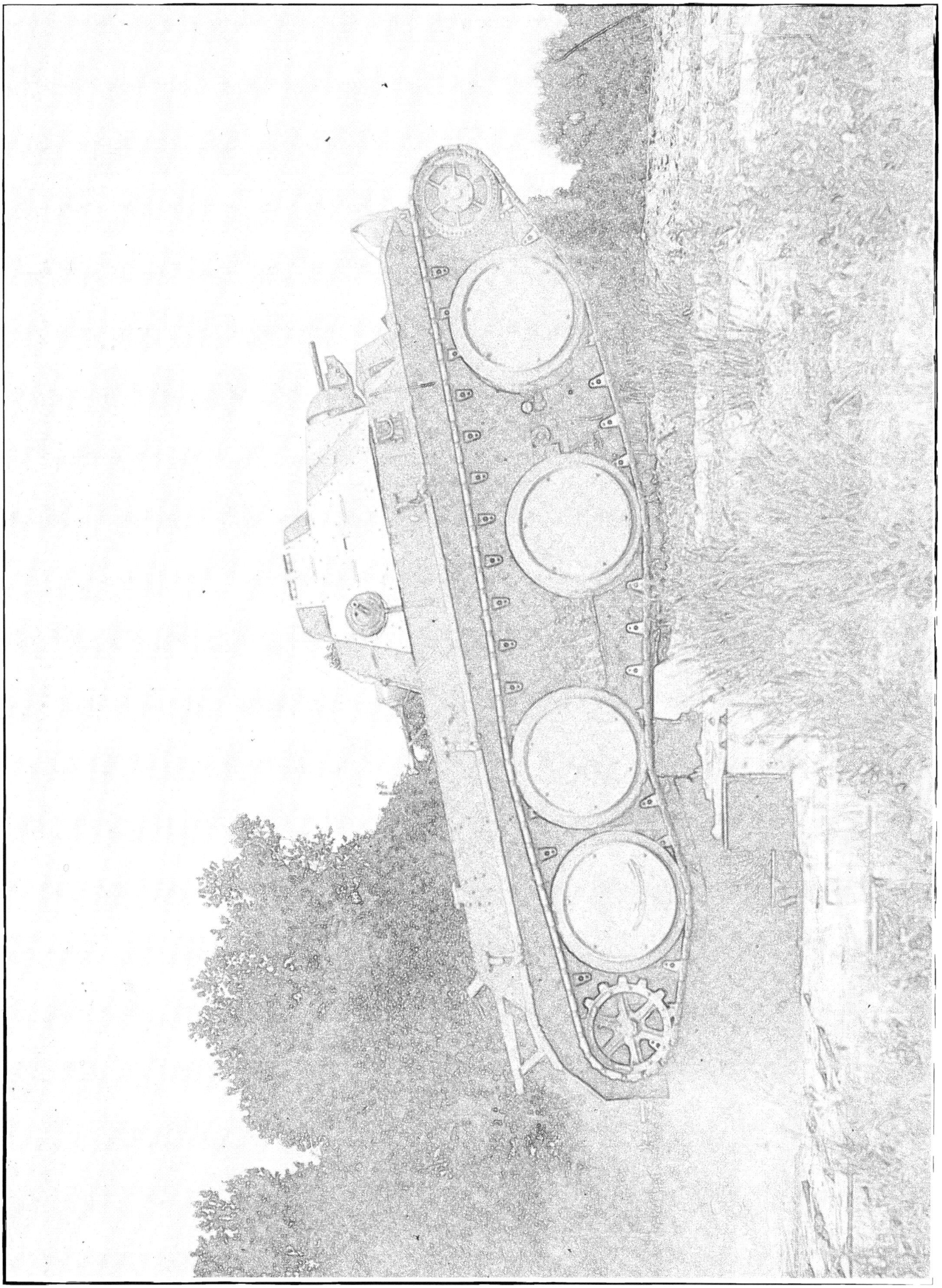

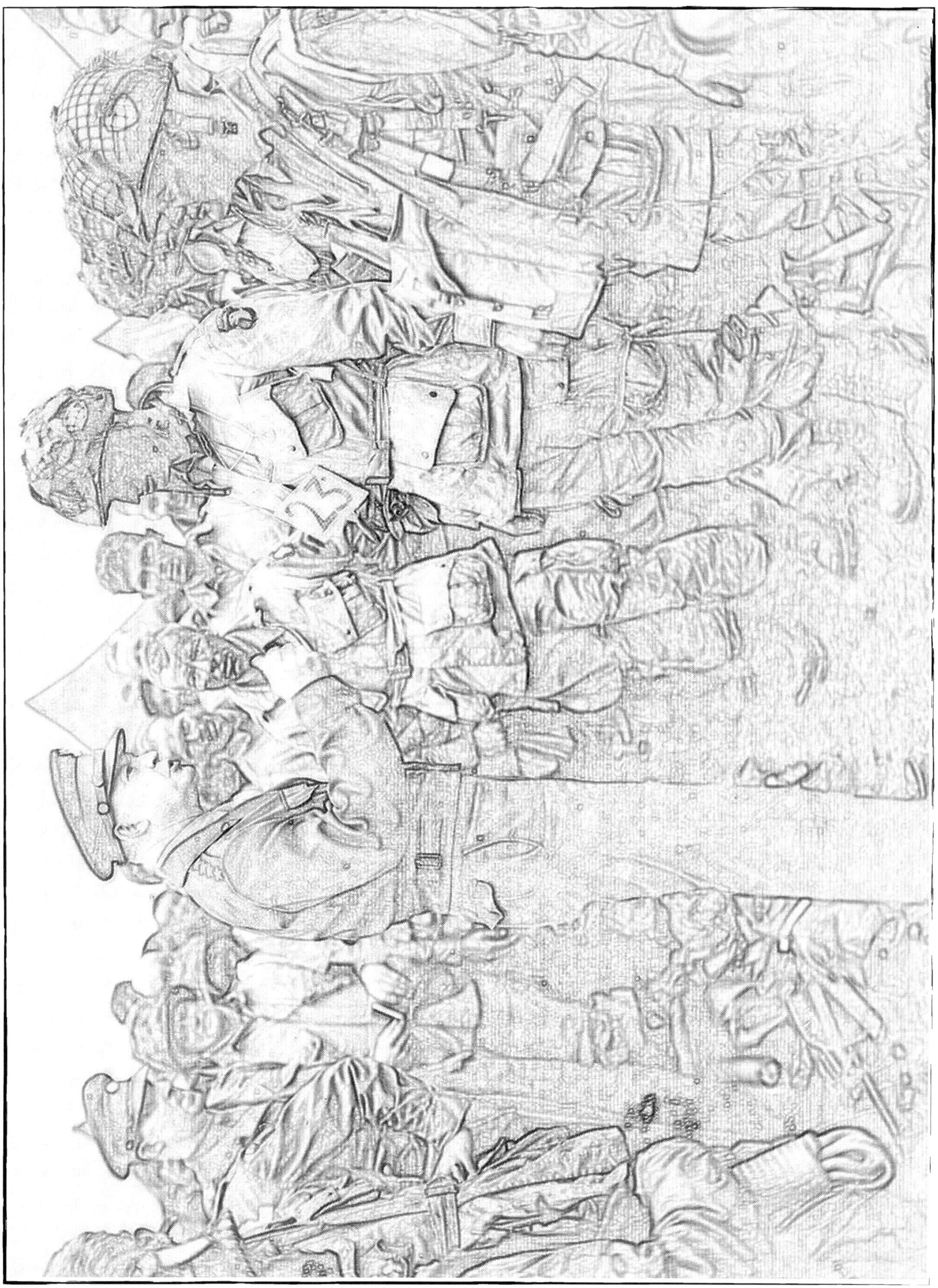

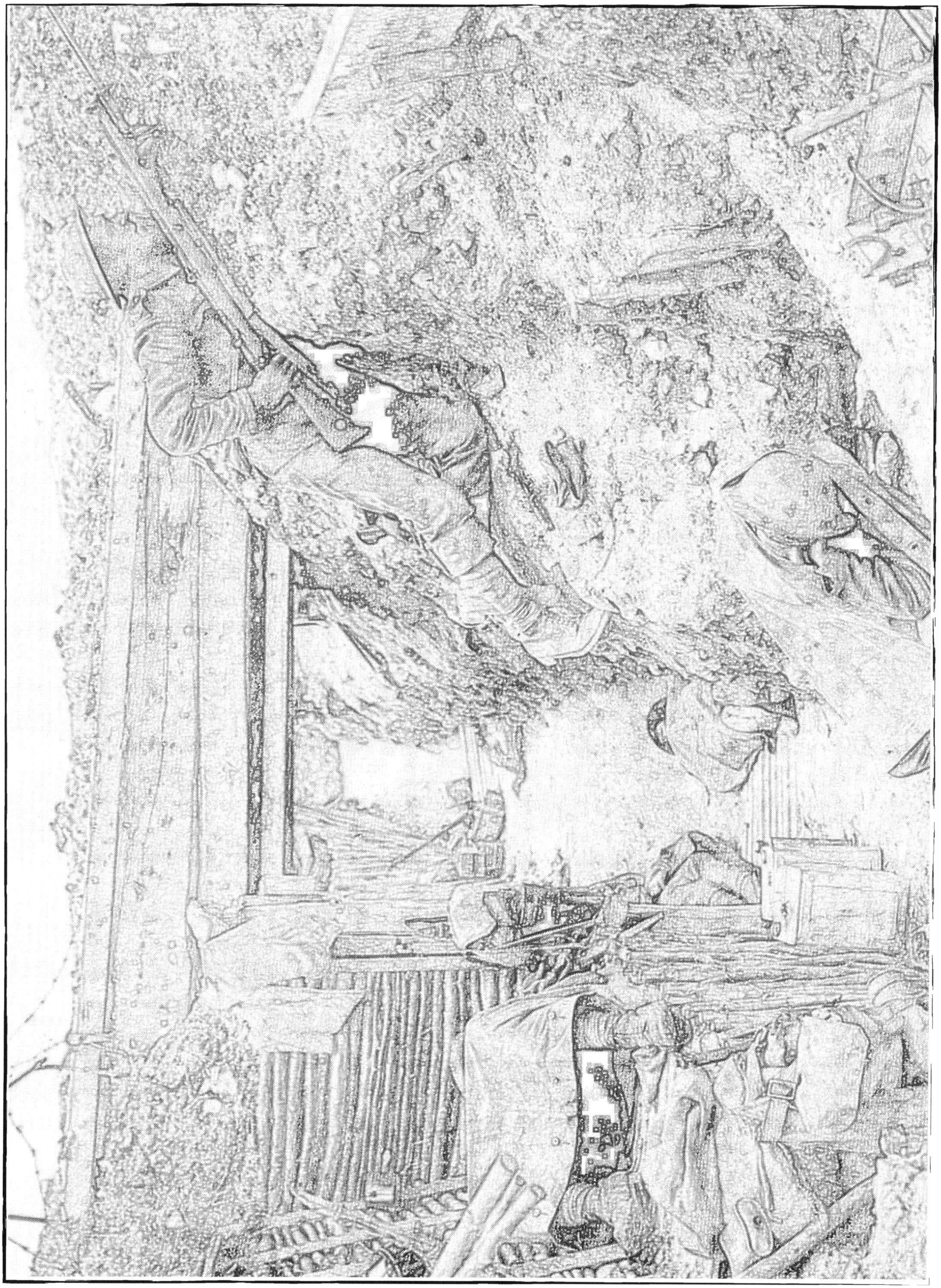

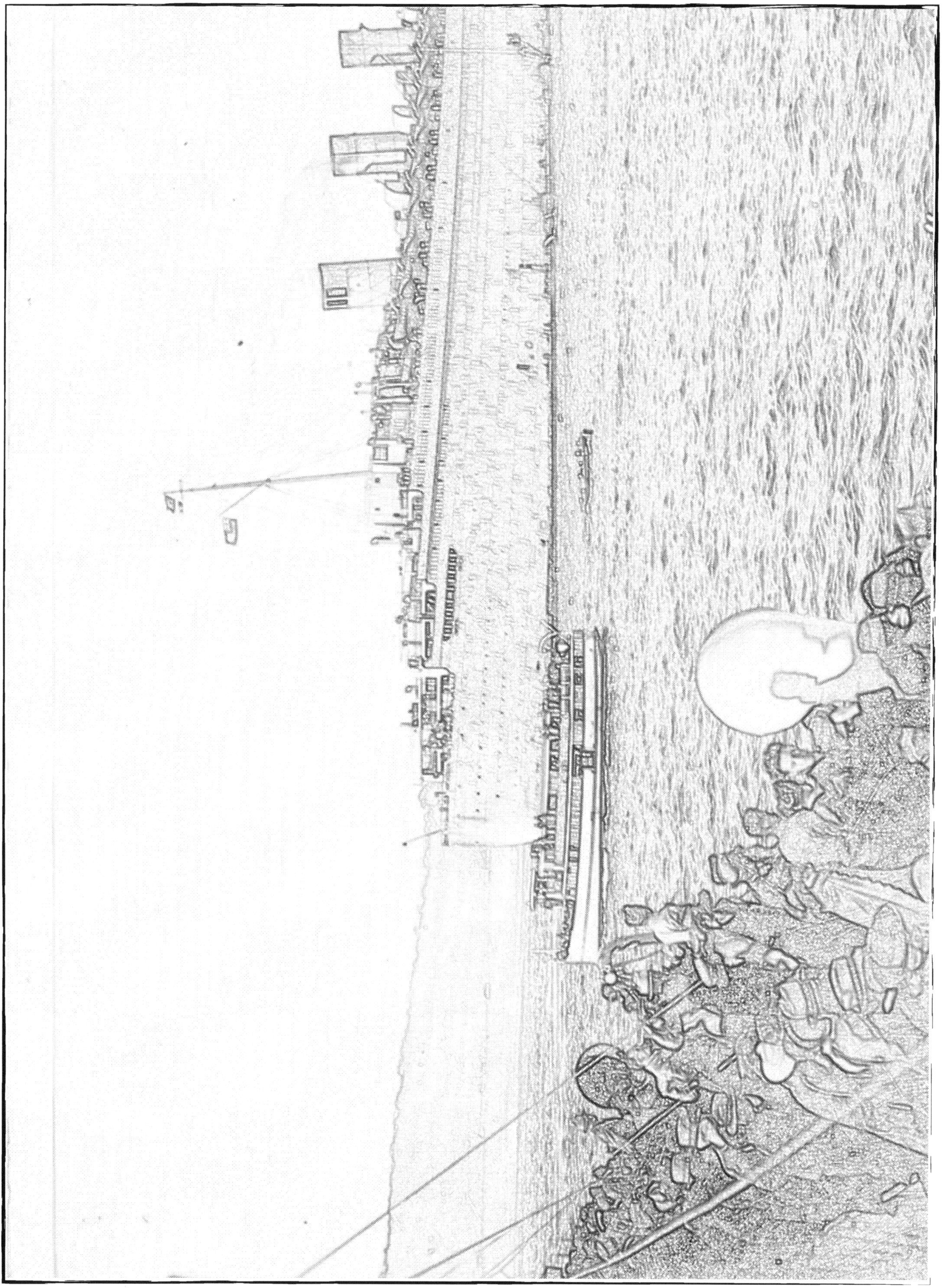

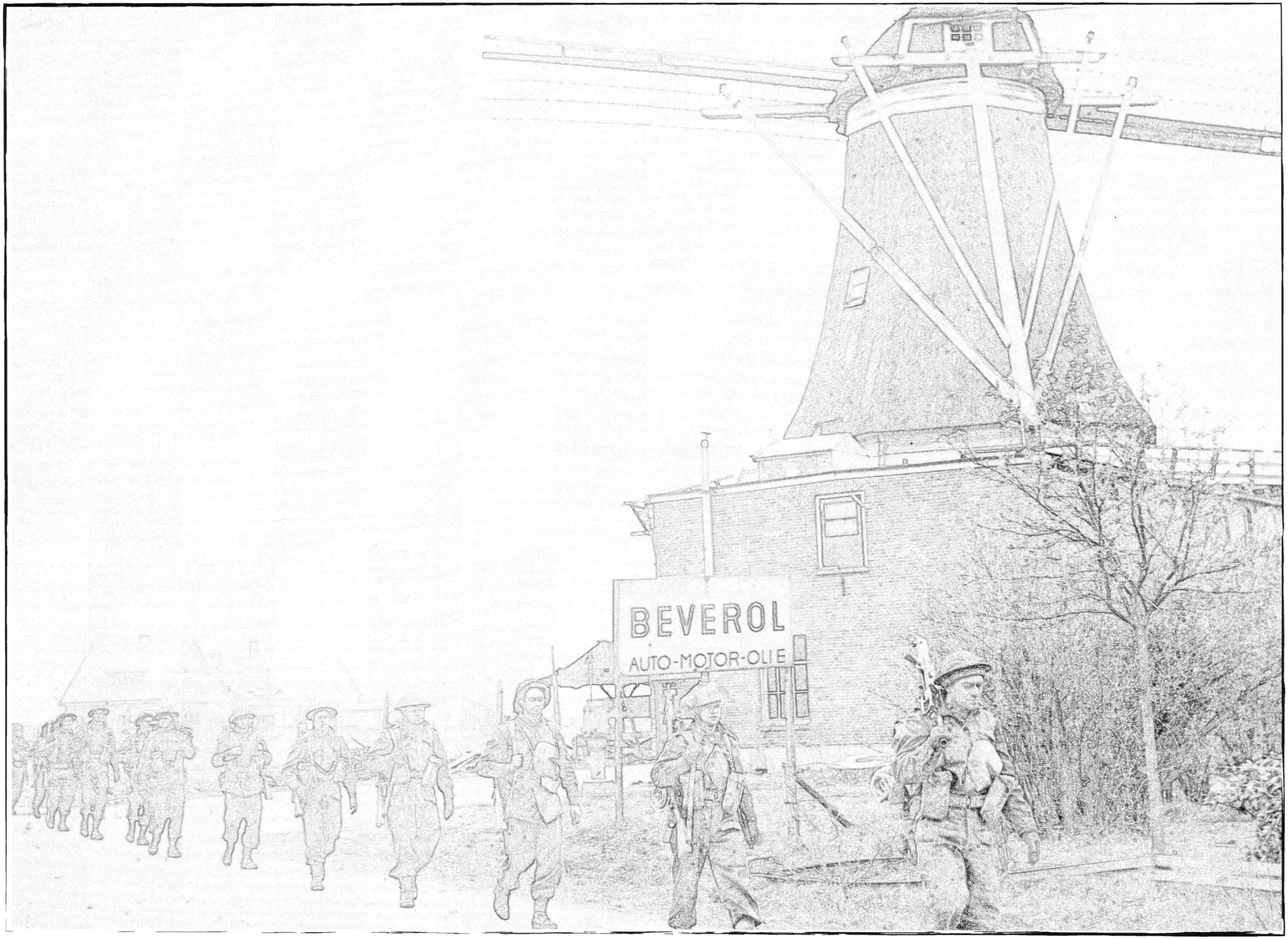
BEVEROL
AUTO-MOTOR-OLIE

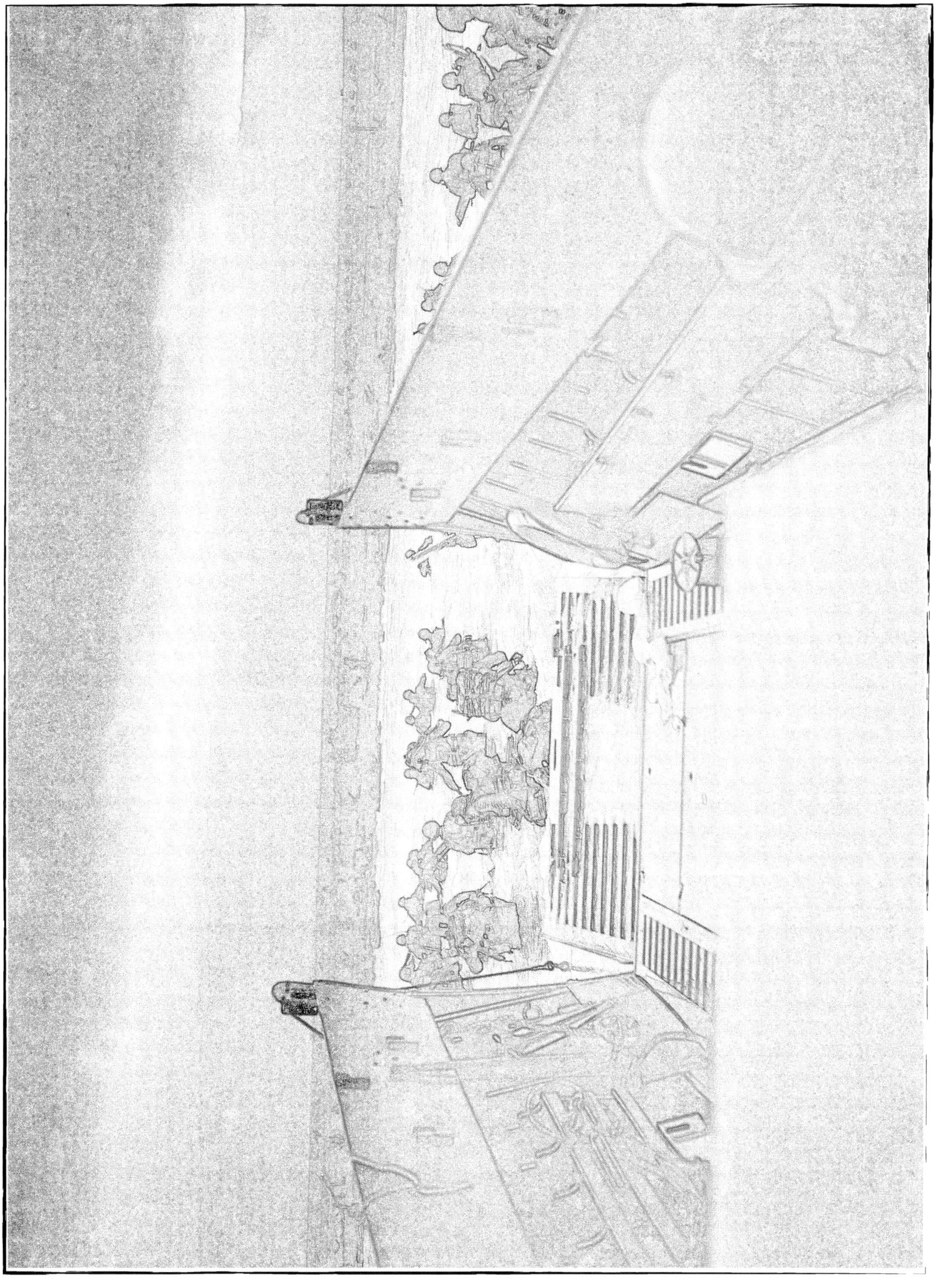

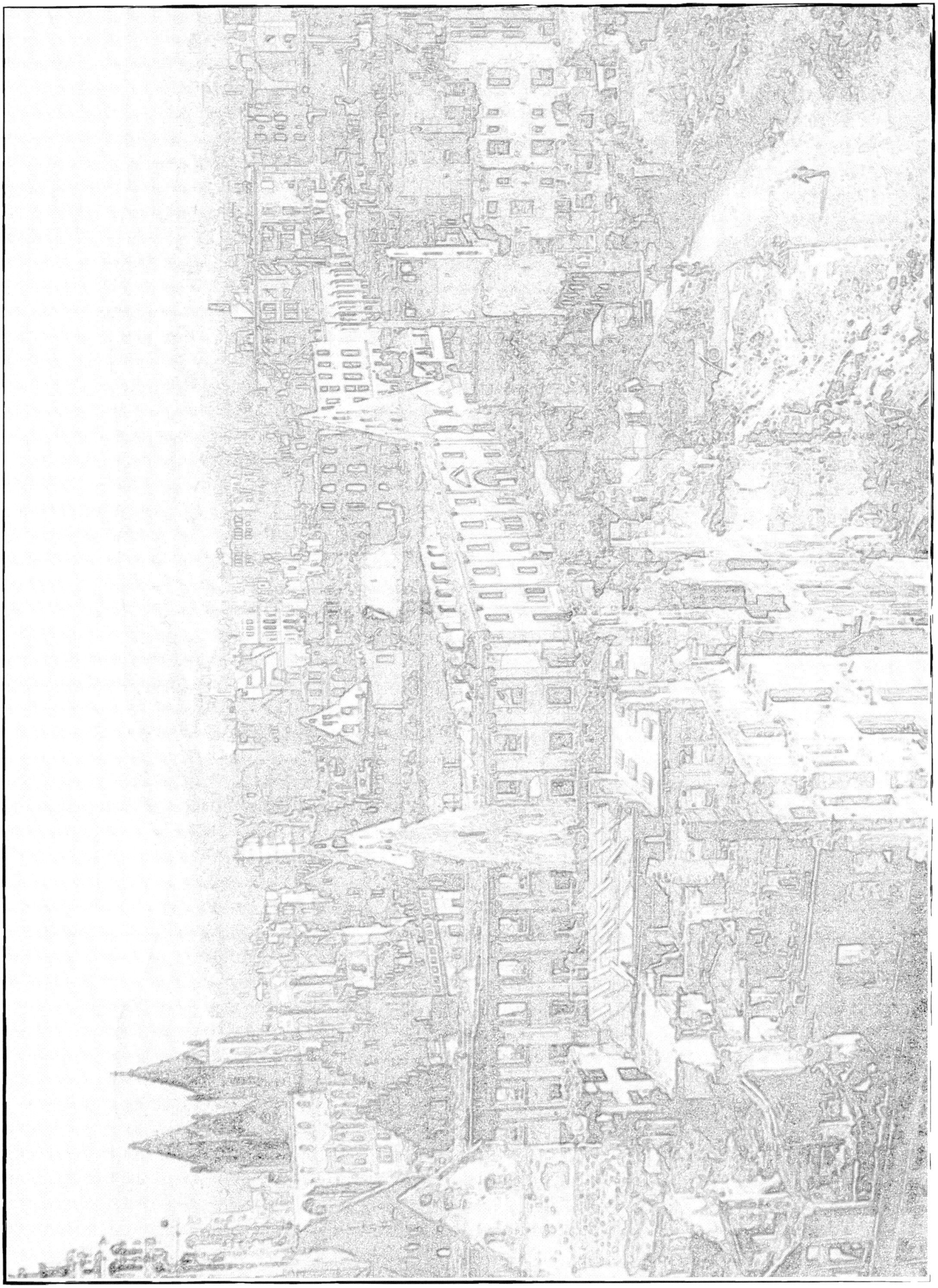

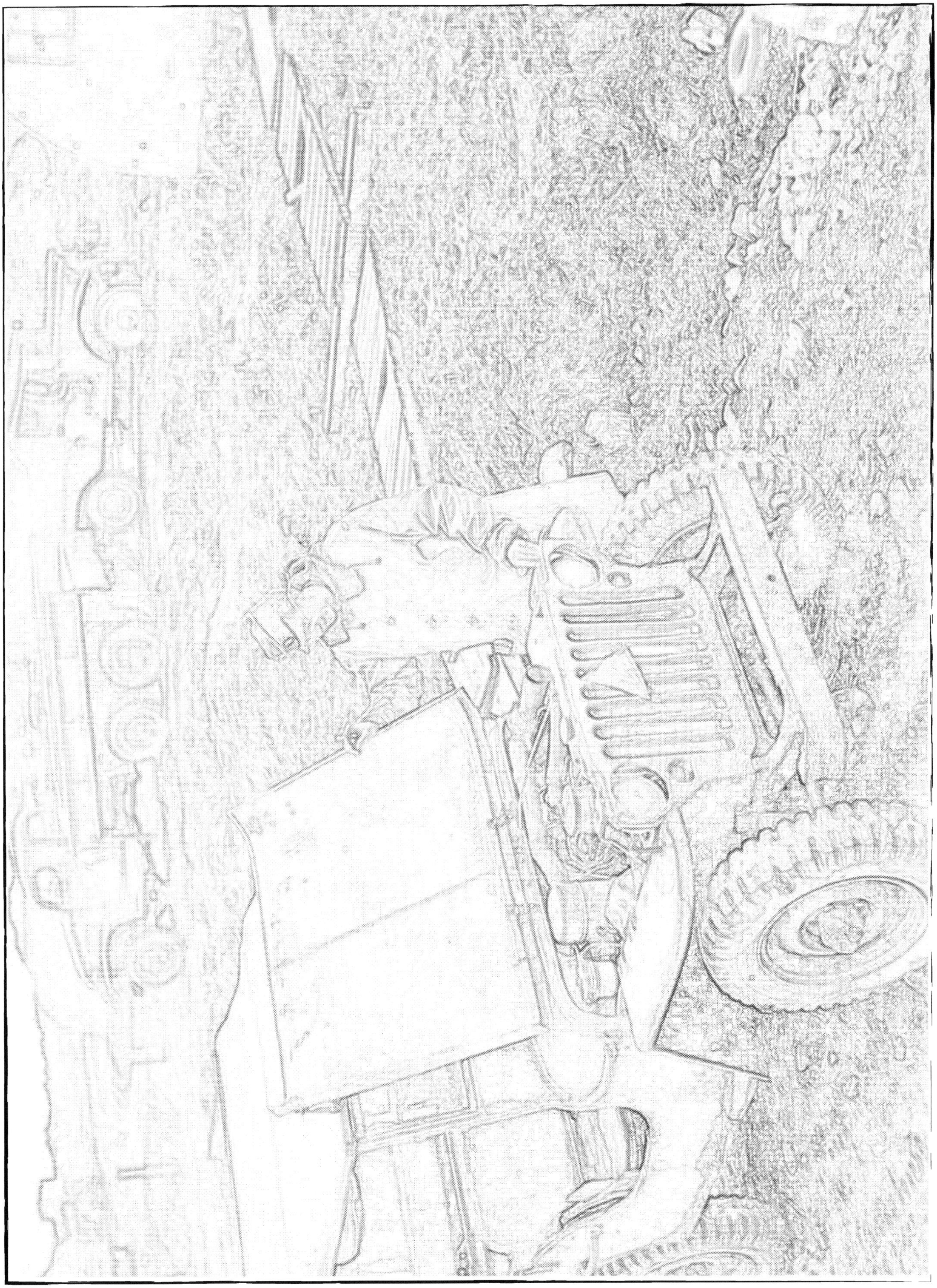

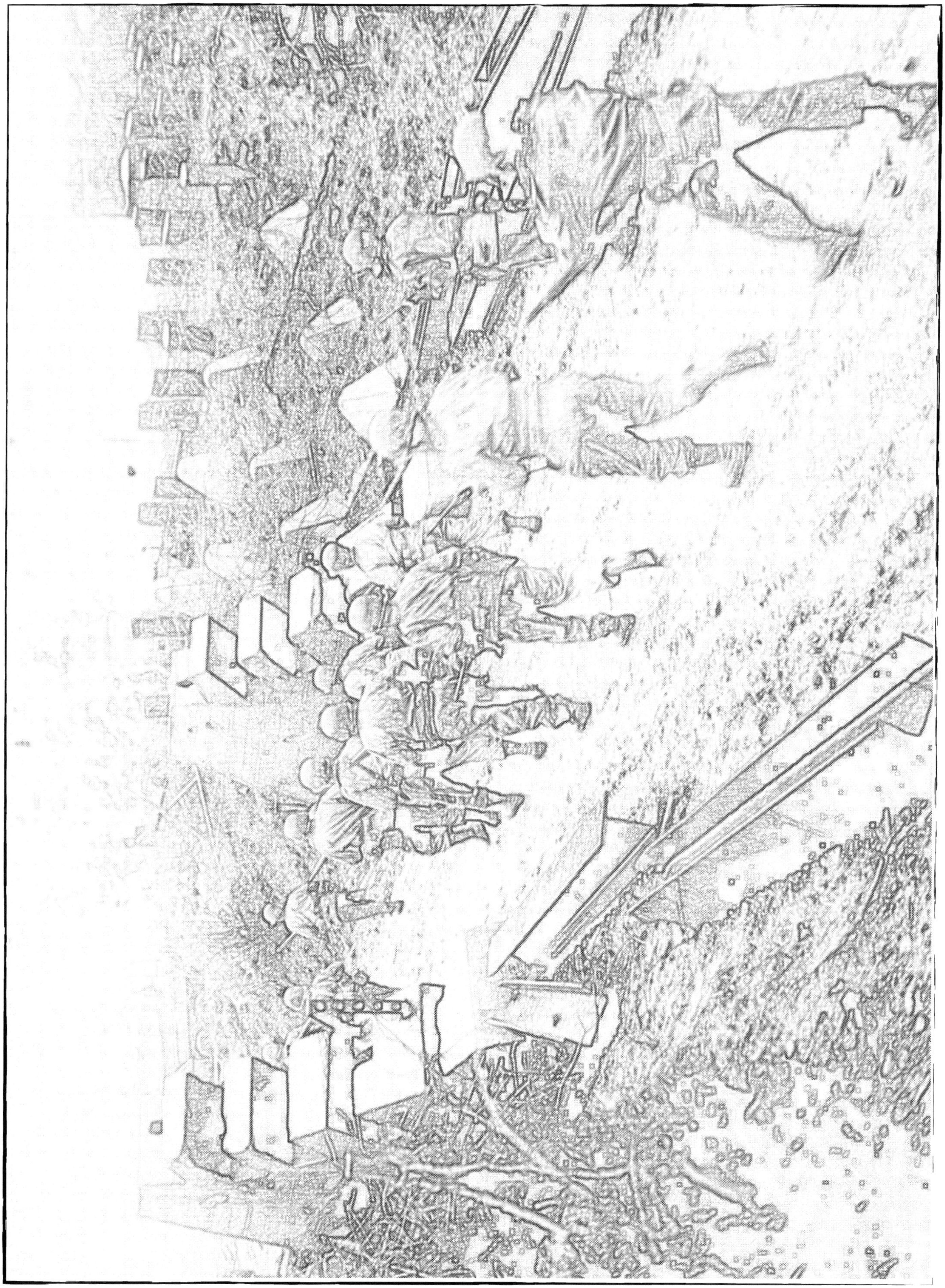

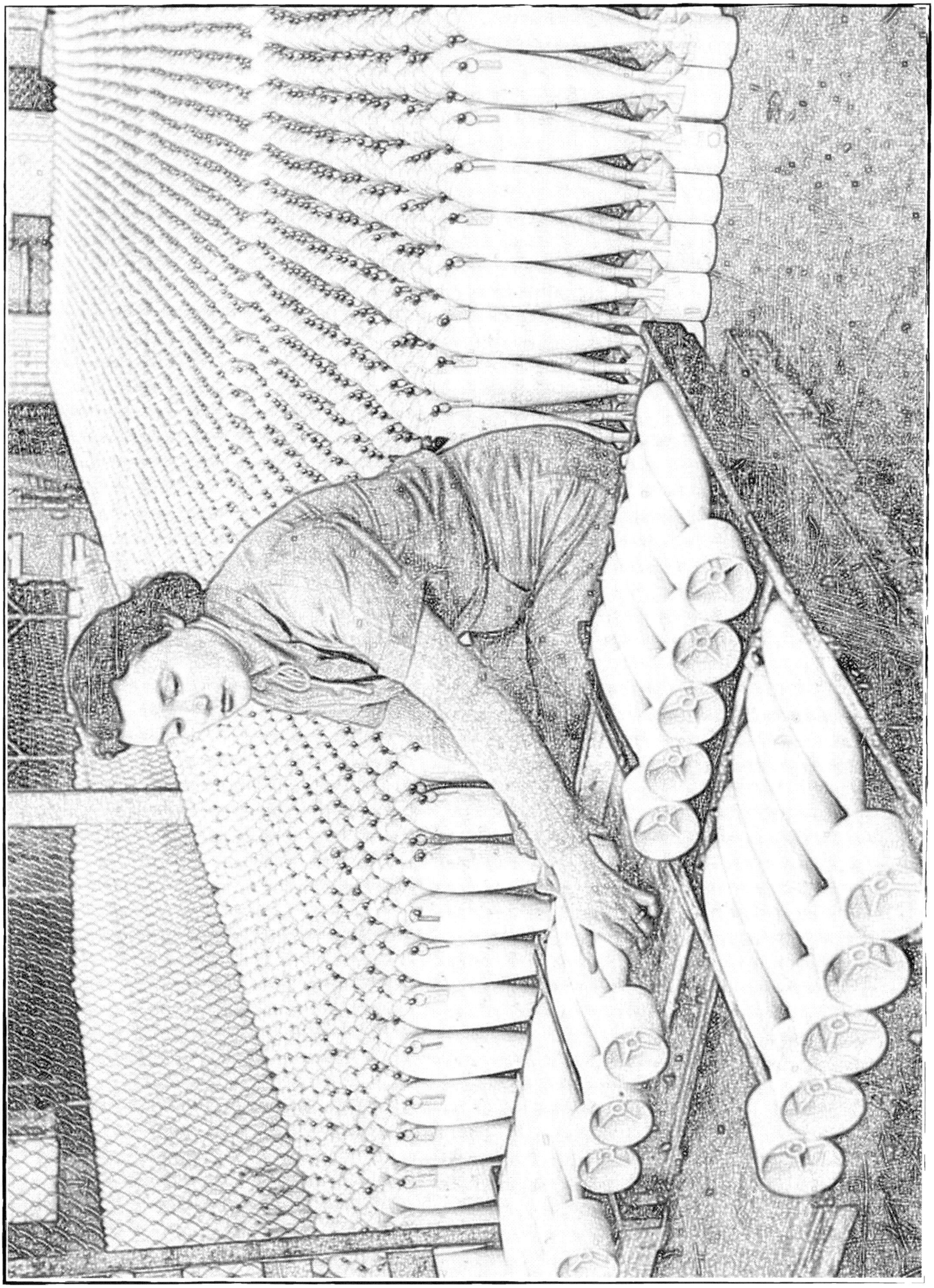

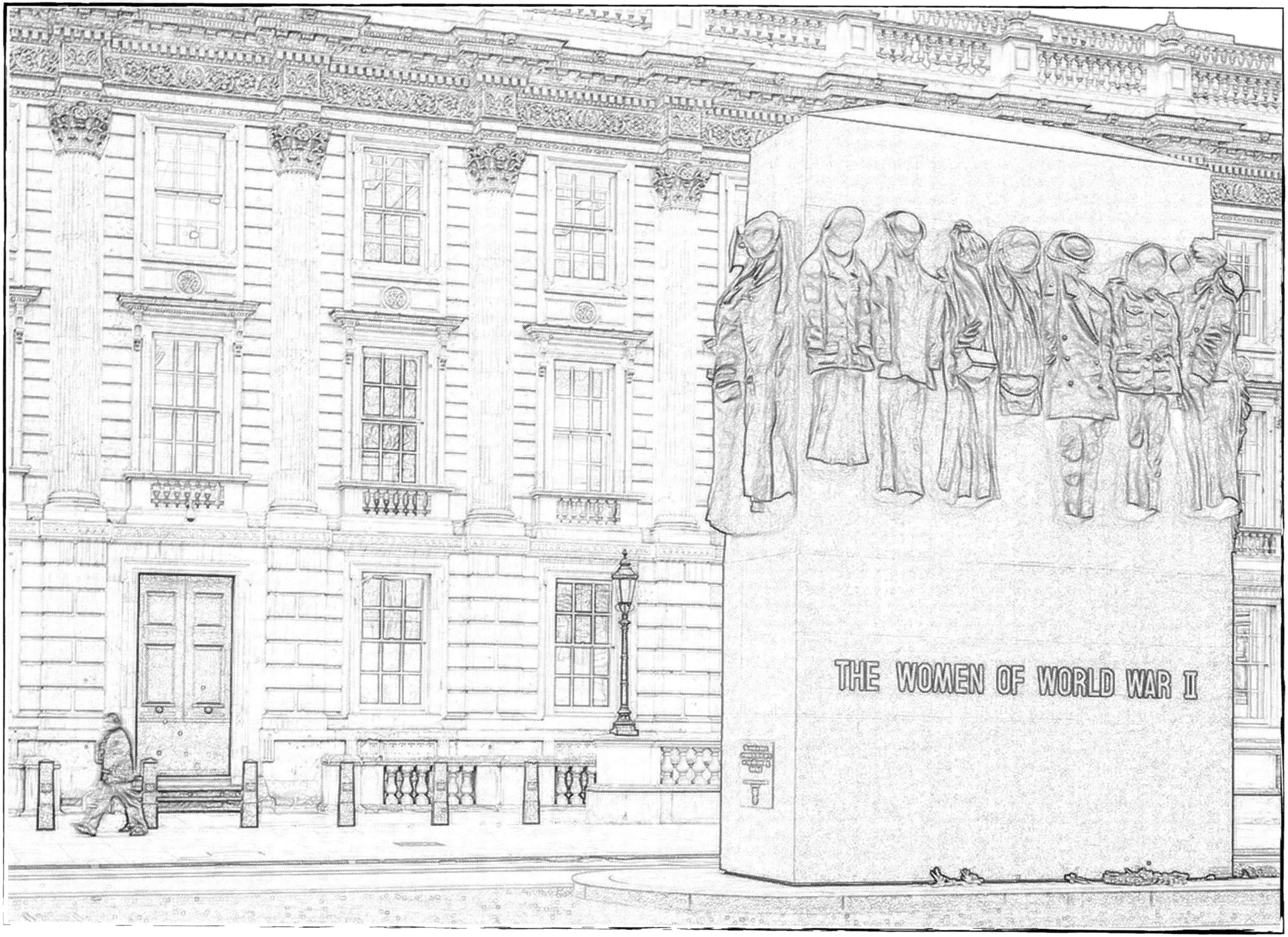
THE WOMEN OF WORLD WAR II

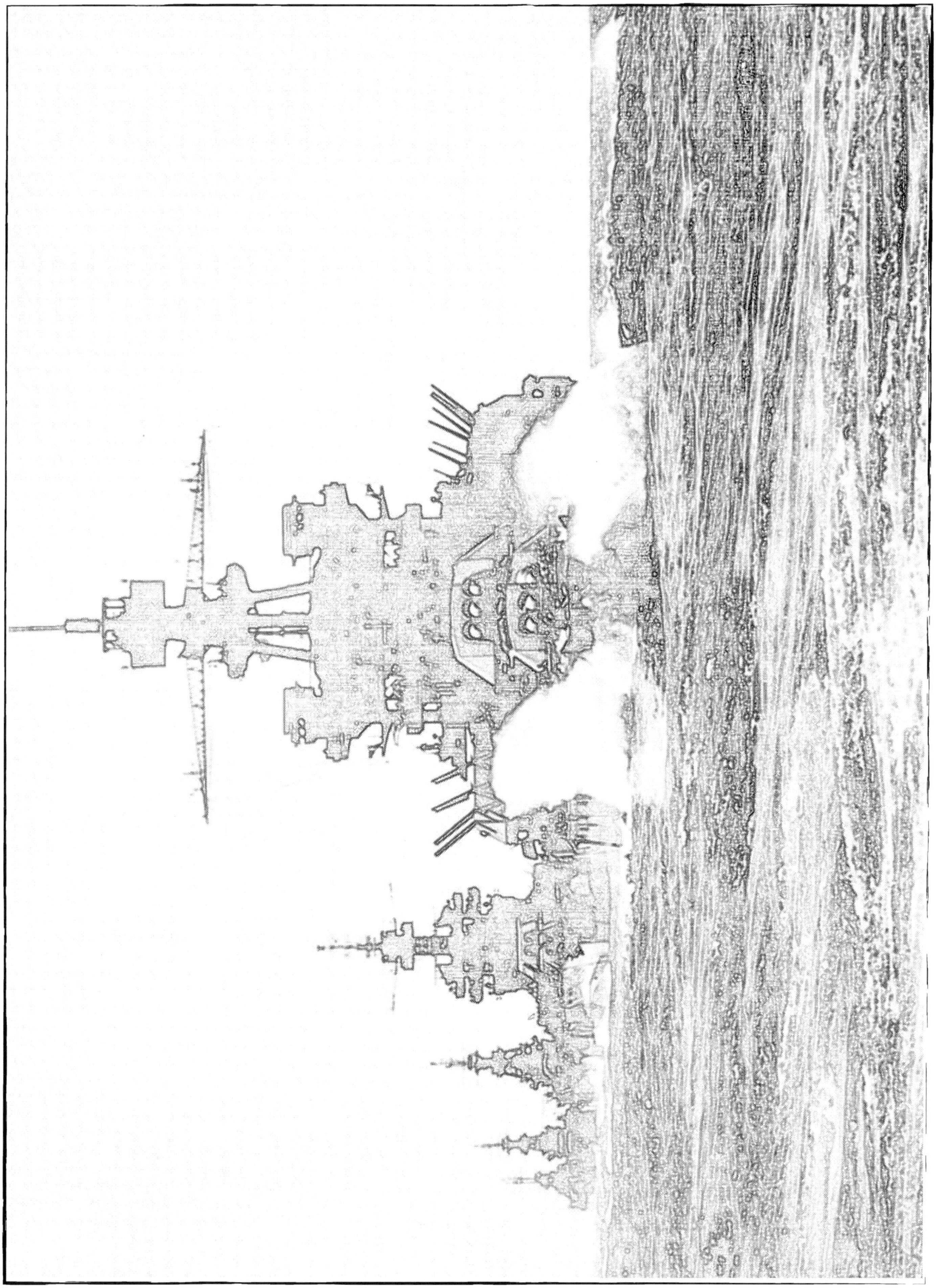

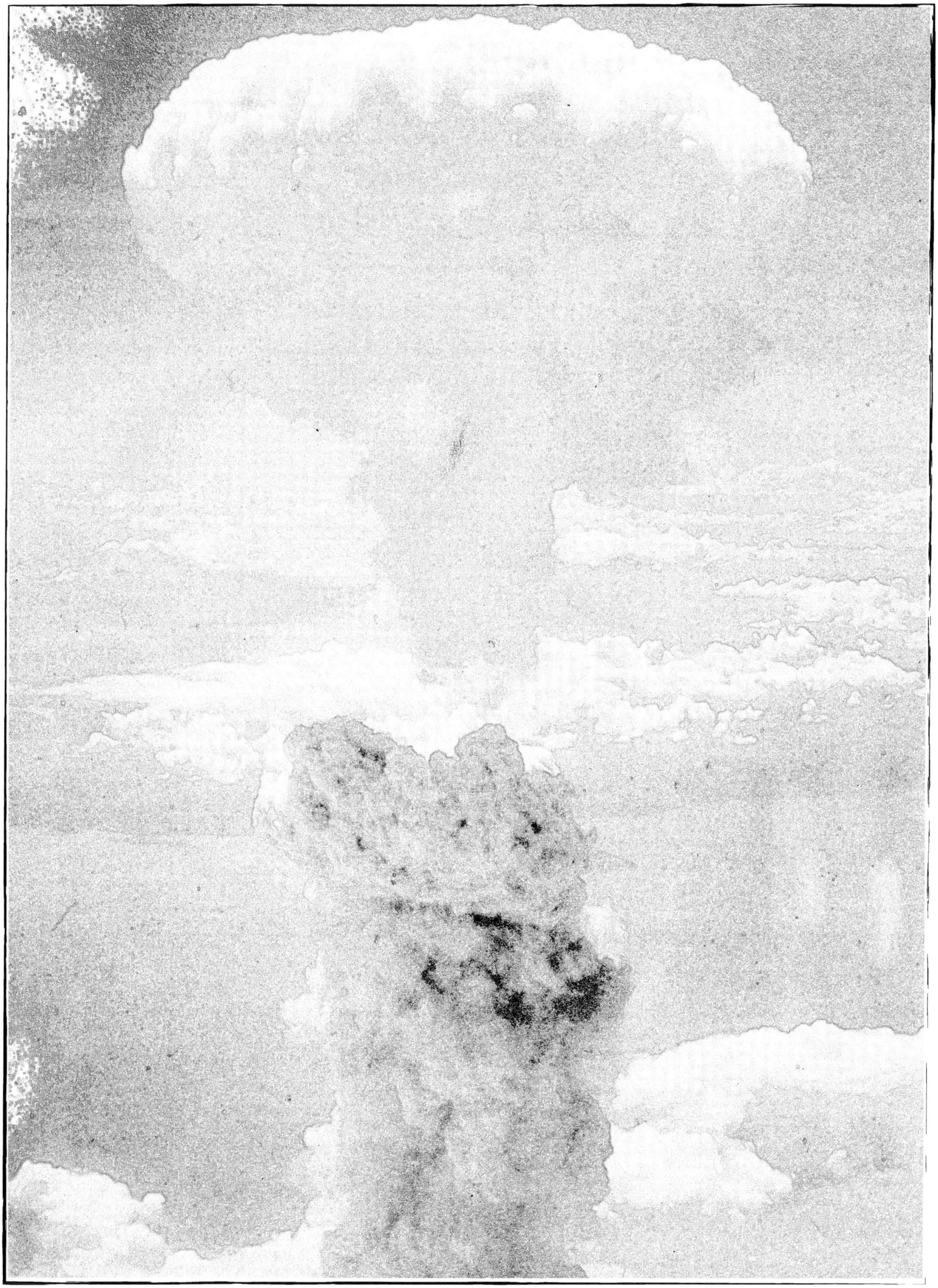

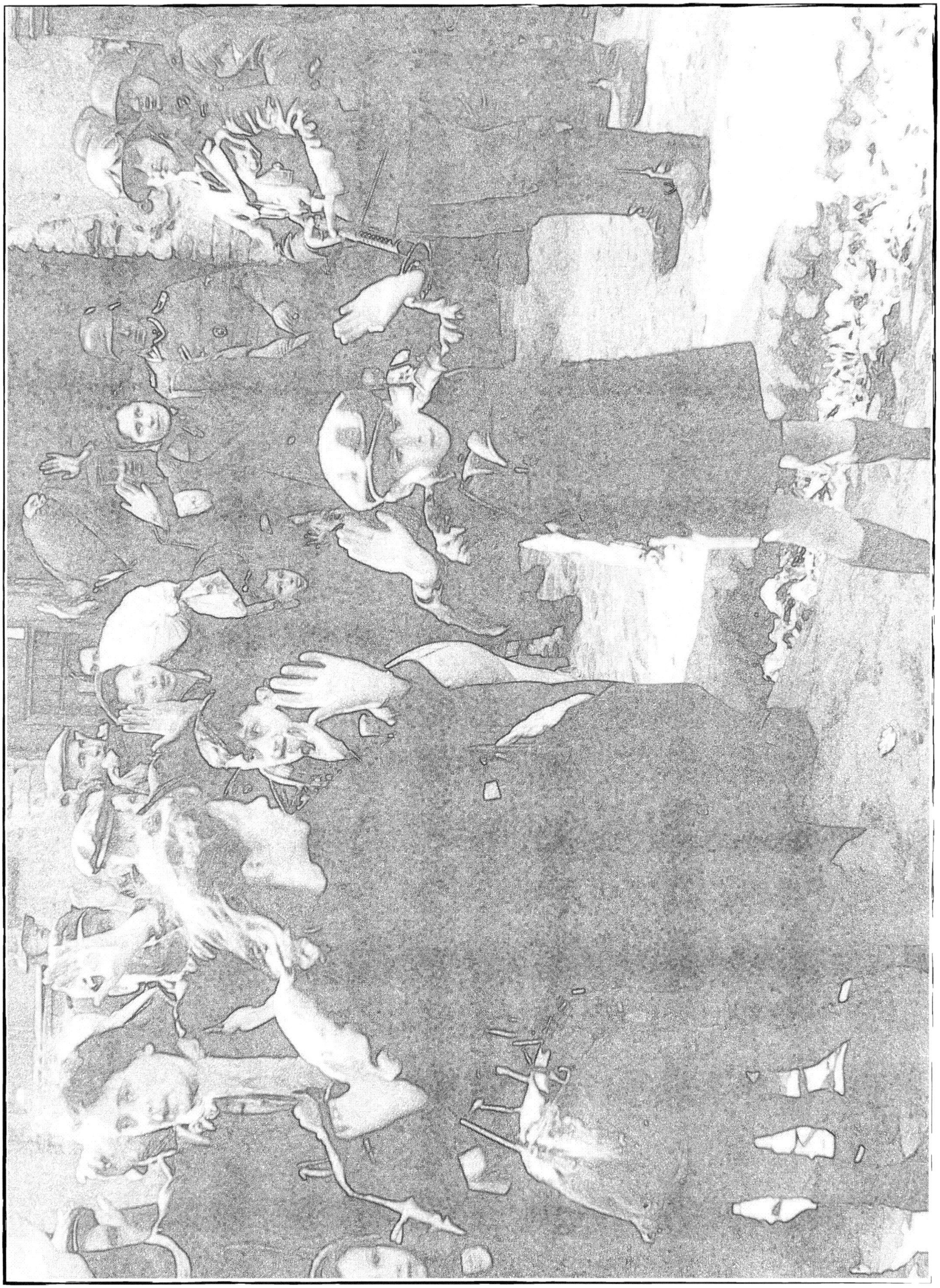

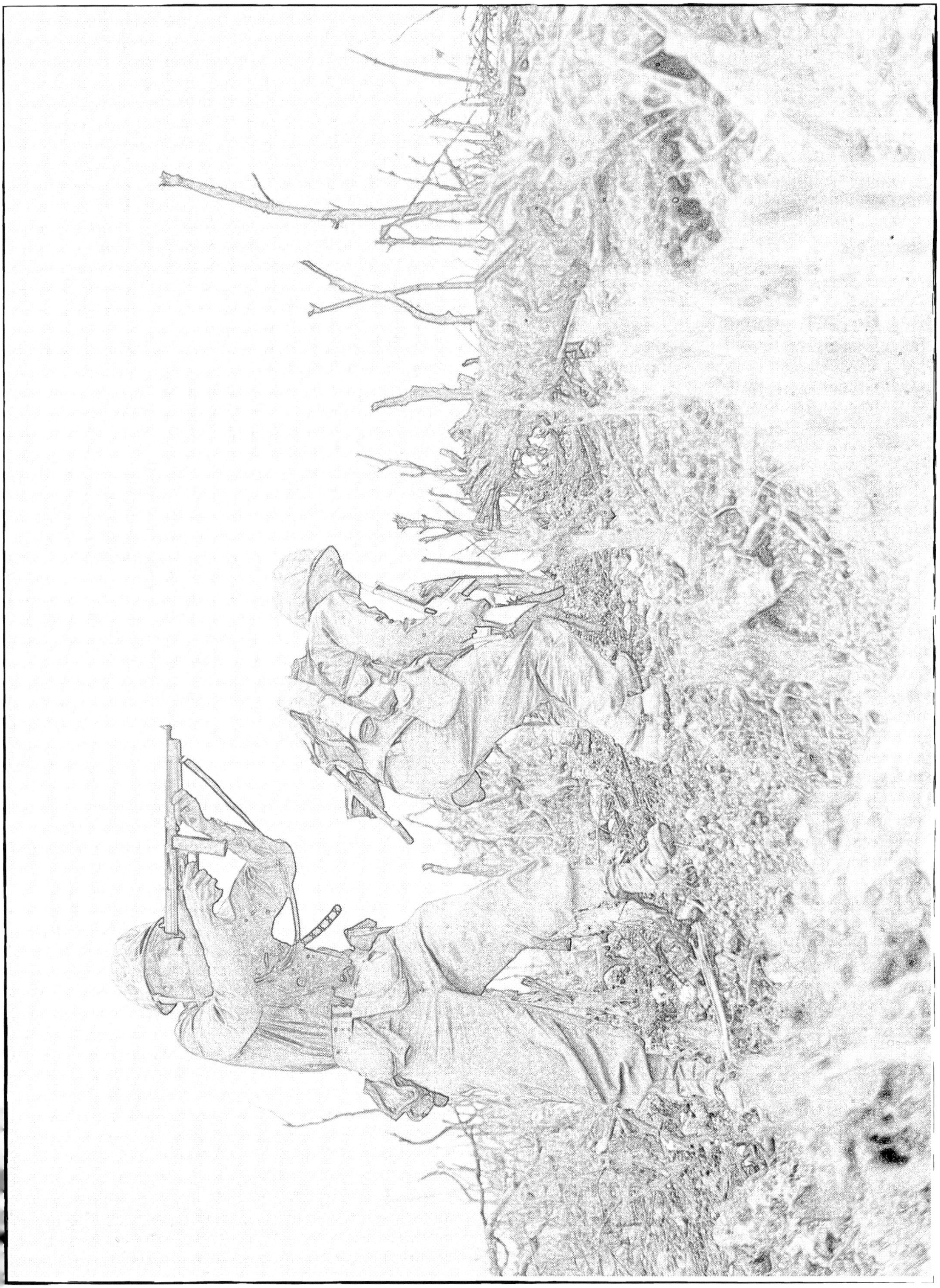

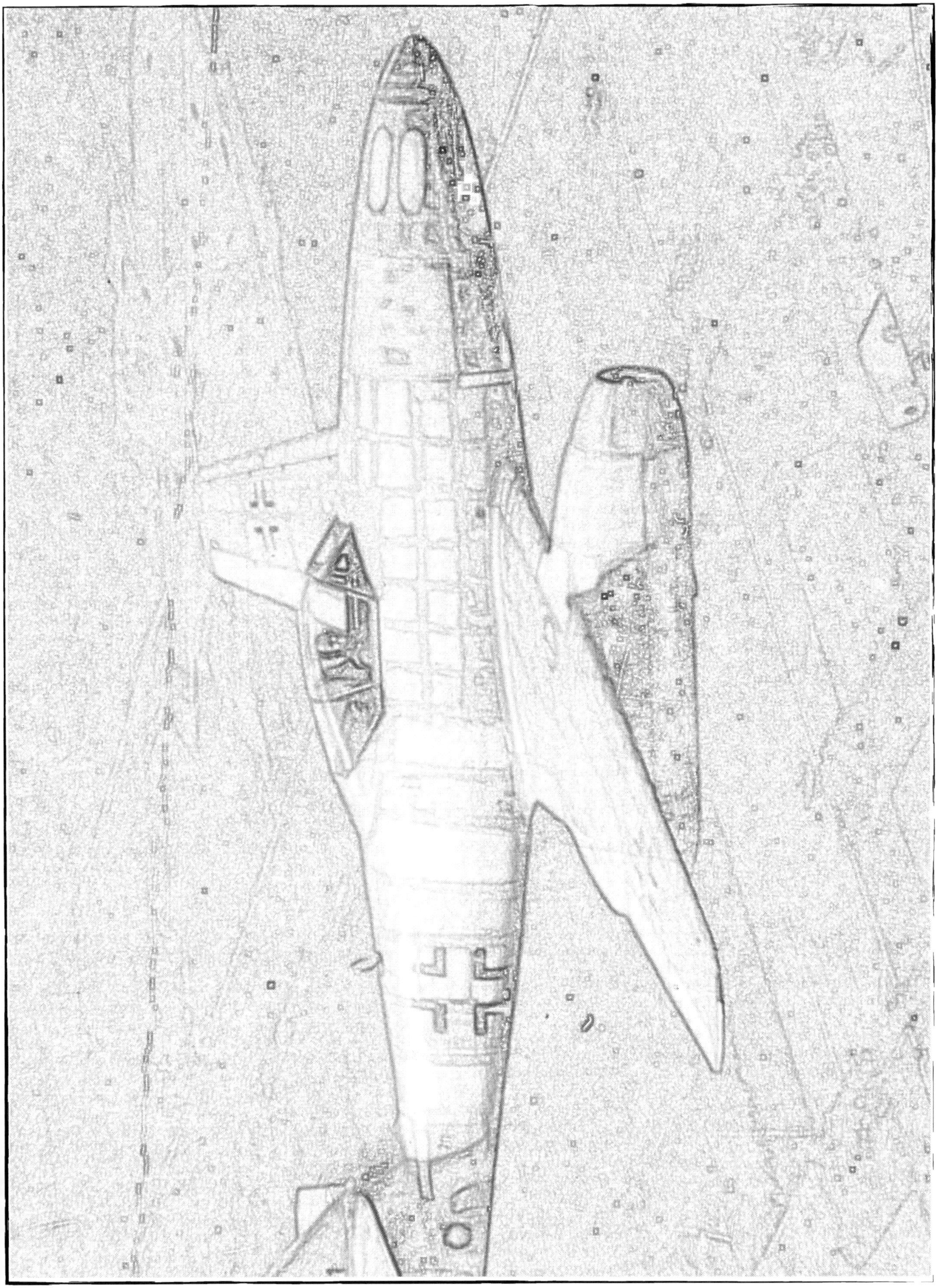

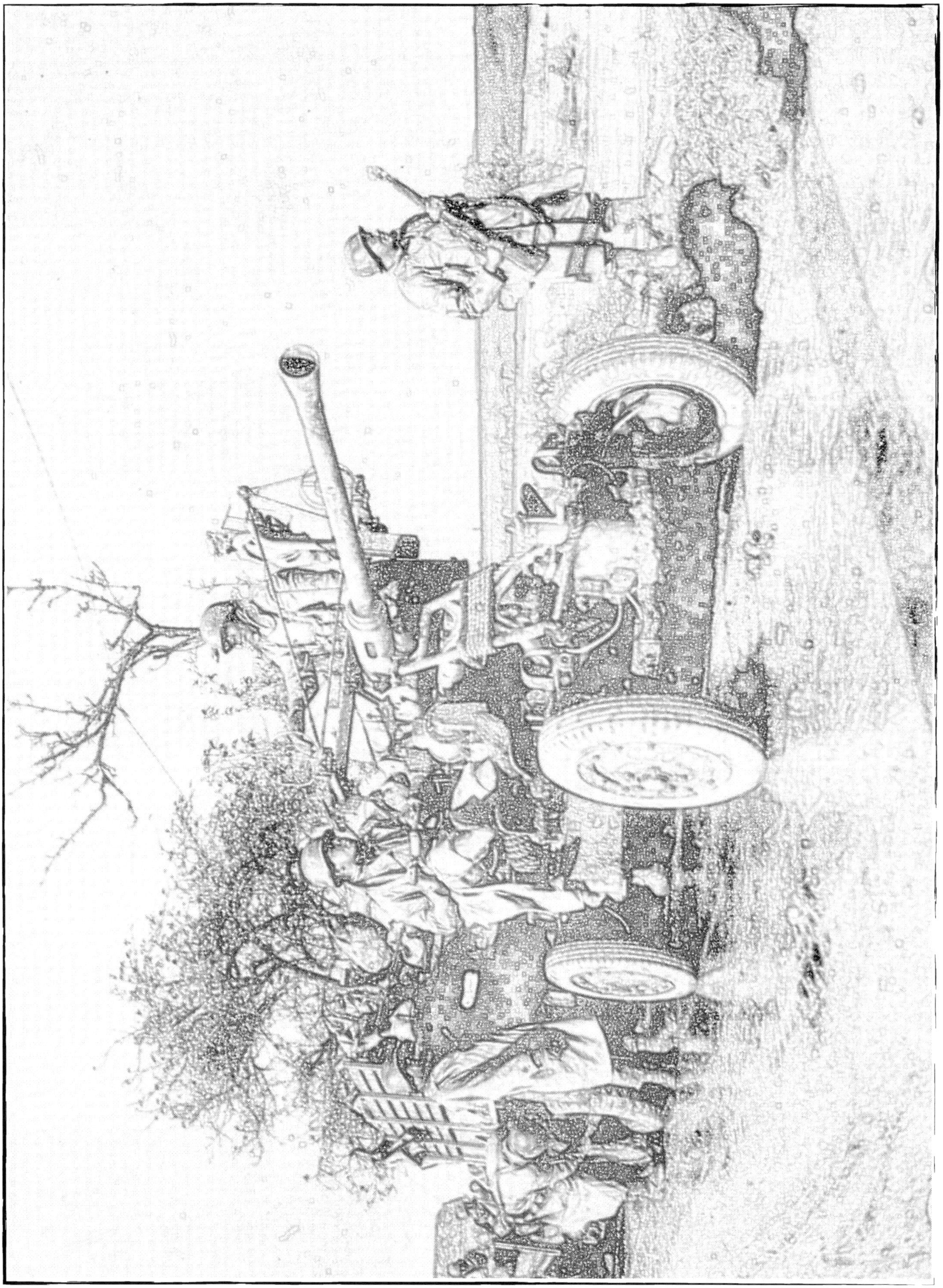

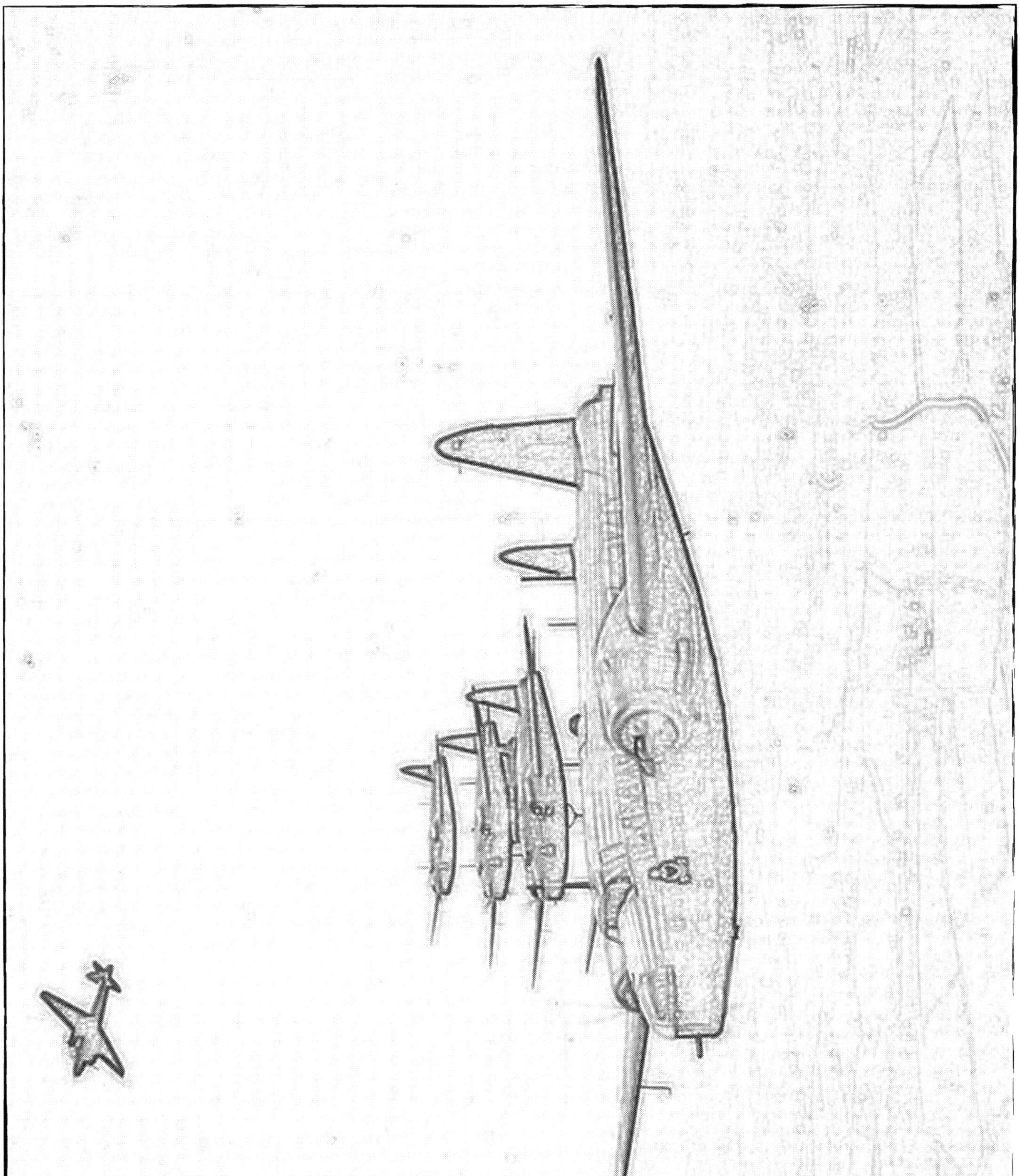

Printed in Great Britain
by Amazon

64853578R00036